MORAL THEOLOGY RENEWED

COLLECTED PAPERS OF THE MAYNOOTH UNION SUMMER SCHOOLS

Mother of the Redeemer, edited by Kevin McNamara, Gill & Son: Dublin 1959; Sheed & Ward: New York 1960. Papers of the 1958 session.

Preaching, edited by Ronan Drury, Gill & Son: Dublin 1962; Sheed & Ward: New York 1963. Papers of the 1960 session.

Christian Unity, edited by Kevin McNamara, The Furrow Trust, Gill & Son: Dublin 1962. Papers of the 1961 session.

The Meaning of Christian Marriage, edited by Enda McDonagh, The Furrow Trust, Gill & Son: Dublin 1963; Alba House: New York 1964. Papers of the 1962 session.

Sacraments, edited by Denis O'Callaghan, The Furrow Trust, Gill & Son: Dublin 1964; Sheed & Ward: New York 1964. Papers of the 1963 session.

MORAL THEOLOGY RENEWED

Papers of the Maynooth Union Summer School 1964

EDITED BY
ENDA McDONAGH

THE FURROW TRUST
GILL AND SON DUBLIN

First published in 1965 by M. H. Gill and Son Ltd
50 Upper O'Connell Street, Dublin 1
and 28 Burke Street, Melbourne
in association with The Furrow Trust, Maynooth

Nihil Obstat:
EDUARDUS GALLEN
Censor Theol. Deput.

Imprimi Potest:
+ JOANNES CAROLUS
Archiep. Dublinen.
Hiberniæ Primas

Dublini die 1a Novembris, 1965

COVER DESIGN BY DES FITZGERALD

Printed in the Republic of Ireland

CONTENTS

INTRODUCTION 7

MORAL THEOLOGY:
THE NEED FOR RENEWAL
by Enda McDonagh 13

THE LAW, THE PROPHETS AND
THE GOSPEL
by Wilfrid Harrington O.P. 31

THE BLESSED TRINITY AND
THE CHRISTIAN LIFE
by John J. Greehy 55

THE LAW OF CHRIST
by Joseph Fuchs S.J. 70

LIFE IN CHRIST:
LIFE IN THE CHURCH
by Kevin McNamara 85

THE MASS IN THE CHRISTIAN LIFE
by Dermot Ryan 103

THE PRIMACY OF CHARITY
by Enda McDonagh 130

THE MEANING OF JUSTICE
by Denis O'Callaghan 151

SIN AND REPENTANCE
by Cornelius Williams O.P. 173

SELECT BIBLIOGRAPHY 195

CONTRIBUTORS

The Reverend Josef Fuchs, S.J., is Professor of Moral Theology at the Gregorian University in Rome.

The Reverend John J. Greehy is Professor of Sacred Scripture at Oscott College, Birmingham.

The Reverend Wilfrid Harrington, O.P., is Professor of Sacred Scripture at Saint Mary's, Tallaght.

The Reverend Enda McDonagh is Professor of Moral Theology at Saint Patrick's College, Maynooth.

The Reverend Kevin McNamara is Professor of Dogmatic Theology at Saint Patrick's College, Maynooth.

The Reverend Denis O'Callaghan is Professor of Moral Theology at Saint Patrick's College, Maynooth.

The Reverend Dermot Ryan is Professor of Oriental Languages at University College, Dublin.

The Reverend Cornelius Williams, O.P., is Professor of Moral Theology at the University of Fribourg.

INTRODUCTION

In accord with its policy of bringing its members abreast of current theological developments, the Maynooth Union Summer School devoted its seventh session (August 1964) to renewal in moral theology. In a tradition where regular confession is emphasized and practised (as a feature of English-speaking Catholicism, sometimes called *Catholicisme du type Irlandais)* the major developments in moral theology which have been taking place in the recent years are of immediate and practical interest. The unusually large attendance and lively discussions at the School confirmed this.

In planning the programme of lectures, the committee was primarily concerned with restoring moral theology to its true theological sources in revelation and scripture. It was for that reason that of the eight lecturers invited to speak, three were scripture scholars and one a dogmatic theologian. The original and more intimate relationship between scripture, dogmatic theology and moral theology was emphasized at the expense of the conventional alliance between moral theology and canon law. Because moral theology was first of all theology, it was felt necessary to investigate and demonstrate this and to refuse to allow it to be absorbed by the concepts and categories of a human legal tradition.

The first lecture ' The Need for Renewal ' attempts to establish the basis of the new approach to moral theology. The necessity for rethinking moral theology arises not at the level of the superficial unattractiveness of the moral manuals with their legal categories and negative emphasis but at the very radical level of the nature of theology. Christian theology is a scientific study of God's self-revelation in Christ conducted subject to Christ's teaching authority now exercised in his Church. This study as St Thomas insisted, enjoys a unity which should never be forgotten. However it is convenient to call the study of that revelation as a system of truth dogmatic theology and to take as moral theology the study of it as a way of life or mode of behaviour. The divine intervention and self-revelation in human history was not given simply for its own sake but as an invitation to man to share the divine life. In Christ the God-man that invitation was manifested most fully and the human response achieved its supreme expression. And it is this invitation-response structure which underlies and informs the whole Christian life of man and the scientific study of it in Christian moral theology. To make the divinely-revealed truths and the divine structure of man's life and behaviour evident is the basic aim of the present efforts at renewal.

The God-man relationship embodied in this invitation-response structure has a history. The second lecture, ' The Law, the Prophets and the Gospel ' uses the more important stages of that history to outline God's way of life for his people until it reaches its climax in Christ and his Church. The abolition and fulfilment of the old law which was the mission of Christ indicates the radical change which his coming accomplished and at the same time the continuity of the divine plan. It is the misunderstanding of this paradox which is at the source of these two most common forms of deviation in Christian moral thinking, that of legalism (the Catholic temptation with its exaggeration of the continuity and its minimizing of the radical renewal) and that of an ethics of inspiration (the Protestant temptation with its exaggeration of the renewal and neglect of the continuity).

In the climactic intervention of God through Christ, the intimate divine reality was finally revealed as comprising three distinct persons within the single Godhead. It was in their respective rôles in the invitation-response structure that the three divine persons were revealed. The Father as initiator of the plan for man's salvation sent the Son who in becoming man provided the way for divine-human contact in invitation and response. By union with the Son man is enabled to respond. But this response is elicited under the power of the Spirit whom the Son promised on his return to the Father and by whose power indeed the Son first took flesh in the womb of the Virgin Mary. The rôle of the three persons in the salvation of the race as a whole is lived out in the invitation to and response of each individual. The immediate scriptural foundation for this in St Paul and St John forms the topic of Father Greehy's 'The Blessed Trinity and the Christian Life.'

Christ as God made man provides the key to the Christian life. In him the full manifestation of the divine as invitation is met by the complete response of man. By sharing in this Christ-life, each man utters his own response in accordance with that *lex gratiae—lex indita* of which St Augustine and St Thomas spoke, the law impressed on man's heart by his being remade, born again in the likeness of Christ. Father Fuchs' discussion of this basic source of Christian behaviour makes his paper on 'The Law of Christ' the theological centre of the book.

Union with Christ must be in and with a community, the new people of God, the body of Christ. The implications of this are traced by Father McNamara in the following paper 'Life in Christ: Life in the Church.' The community is a covenant community, brought into being by the new covenant foretold by Jeremias and accomplished in Christ. The sacrifice by which that covenant was first accomplished is realized anew in the Mass for the local community as the means of expression and development of their destiny as God's people. Through the power of this covenant sacrifice and meal, the people are enabled to recognize and fulfil their obligations as God's people. Hence the importance of Father Ryan's talk on 'The Mass in the Christian Life.'

The union with Christ in community and the revivifying of

that unity in the covenant sacrifice and meal, demand expression in the community virtues of charity and justice. All Christian action derives from the divine gift of charity, man's sharing in the divine prerogative of life which is best described as ' God abroad in the world.' The claim to being charitable is hypocrisy or self-deception where it does not issue in that minimal respect for human dignity, human rights and needs, which justice commands. So far from there being any conflict between charity and justice, a full human and Christian attitude to other men combines both, as the two lectures devoted to these virtues try to show. And the attitude implicit in the remark ' it binds *only* in charity ' has no place in a renewed moral theology.

The present divine invitation is a reissue of an invitation originally rejected by man. Man has sinned and is in continual danger of doing so. Response really means conversion and the conversion in face of man's history with the residual inner inclinations and external temptations remains a constant demand. By slow, painful giving of himself to God and his fellowman, man overcomes his heritage of sin and achieves the *metanoia* which forms the core of Christ's call. The ' Sin and Repentance ' aspect of the Christian life presented by Father Williams in the final lecture, reveals the particular kind of dynamism characteristic of fallen man. His morality is necessarily one of growth in that he is a material and temporal being as well as a spiritual one, who only gradually discovers and achieves himself in response to God and the neighbour. Because he is also a sinful being, his progress is continually threatened and conditioned by sin and its consequences. At any particular time the response expected of him by God will be related to his stage of development.

In nine lectures only the outlines of a theology of Christian living could be attempted. And because it is the point of departure for any theological exercise and because it was the most obvious deficiency in the manual treatment, the scriptural basis is given priority. This inevitably emphasizes the divine invitation and its objective content at the expense of the human response and its subjective possibilities. The personal character of this response and in particular the fact that it must be lived out of love and in community are given due recognition. And it is hardly necessary to point out that although there is no lecture explicitly devoted to conscience, the stress on the obligation of the individual to respond personally to the divine invitation rules out any kind of moral living by proxy, by passively allowing somebody else to make one's conscience judgments while at the same time recognizing the rôle of the teaching Church in informing his conscience.

However there are two elements connected with the individuality of the invitation and response which would require fuller treatment in a complete outline of moral theology.

The manual tradition concentrated on the universal and essential moral obligations and treated the individual case as merely an instance or particular application of the universal principles and no more than that. In the invitation-response context the individuality of the moral situation becomes more evident. And the possibility of individual, existential moral obligations which are not reducible to or deducible from the universal and essential begins to make sense. With a personal call from God in one's total life and the individual situation, each individual may have obligations not shared with others because they do not arise from the humanity and Christianity which he shares, but from his individual, non-shared unique element as this particular man and Christian. Such obligations could never contradict the 'essential obligations' as the defenders of 'Situation Ethics' maintain. And for the majority of cases the prudent application of the essential may suffice. Yet this personal, individual call to something more may never be ignored so that some treatment of what Karl Rahner calls a 'formal existential ethic' will form part of the moral theology of the future.

In responding to this personal call, each man is conditioned by his own human make-up and his environment. And the modern developments in psychology, sociology and allied sciences revealing the various forces within and without man which influence him and his response, have to be gradually integrated into moral theology. Some of these figured largely in the discussions at the Summer School, but because of the desire and need to make manifest the genuine theological and scriptural character of Christian moral theology, they did not receive the treatment which in a full and renewed moral theology they merit.

In spite then of some inevitable omissions it is hoped that the publication of these papers will be of use to the pastoral clergy and the laity in following and assimilating the current renewal in moral theology.

ENDA McDONAGH

Maynooth

MORAL THEOLOGY: THE NEED FOR RENEWAL

Enda McDonagh

Today we readily admit that the Church, and theology as the servant of the Church, are in constant need of renewal. In its role of faith in search of understanding, theology tries to interpret and present God's revelation of himself in Christ in a way that is intelligible and relevant to the contemporary world. The renewal issues from the tension generated between two forces in the mind of the Church or the theologian, the never-ending quest for a fuller understanding of the Christian message and the need to expound that message in the light of the prevailing ideas, needs and problems of the men of a particular time and place. The task of theology then is to provide the intellectual and scientific basis for a fruitful dialogue between the Word of God and his world.

This task has become more urgent in recent times because of the remarkable progress at the tension points, the Word and the world. The increasing understanding of God's Word which modern biblical scholarship provides, and the radical developments in politics, philosophy, psychology and the physical sciences which this century has witnessed, have placed a great responsibility on the Church and its theologians to keep these two points in fruitful contact. Otherwise the Church will be isolated with a theology that, however rich it is in the biblical scholarship of today or yesterday or the speculative thought of another time and place, will be irrelevant and unintelligible to the man to whom God wishes to speak through the Church today, that is, modern man with his own mental and emotional make-up, his own interests and needs. It will have a non-theology in fact.

Attempts to meet the more urgent demands of renewal in theology have been in existence at least since the beginning of the century, although they suffered a serious set-back at an early stage owing to the excesses of Modernism. Today Vatican II has given a new status and impetus to such attempts, and adopted as its own many of the theological developments which preceded it.

Some of these developments affect moral theology in an intimate way. The purpose of this paper is to outline the reasons why any such renewal should be necessary in moral theology, which seemed to be so clearly and completely presented in the various manuals or *Institutiones Theologiae Moralis*. Apart from particular new problems such as the atomic bomb and the contraceptive pill or some changes in the law about the eucharistic fast and the like, there might not seem to be any room for more radical rethinking and presentation. Yet it is in moral theology that some of the most far-reaching attempts at renewal have been made and some of the most intense controversies have arisen.[1]

[1]There is already a vast literature on this subject. Here I can only indicate a few of the most recent articles. The more important fuller works are referred to later in the article and may be consulted for fuller bibliography.

Cf. Bernhard Häring, C.SS.R., 'Heutige Bestrebungen zur Vertiefung und Erneuerung der Moraltheologie' in *Studia Moralia* I, Roma, 1963.

P. Anciaux, 'Religion et Morale' in *Collectanea Mechlinensia* 49 (1964–5), 409 ff.

P. Delhaye, 'Morale et Moralisme' in *Suppl. La Vie Spirituelle* 70 (1964), 243 ff.

F. Böckle, 'Bestrebungen in der Moraltheologie' in *Fragen der Theologie Heute*, Einsiedeln, 1960.

The most useful single work treating of the different needs and aspects of renewal is still, perhaps, *Moral Chrétienne et Requetes Contemporaines*, Tournai, 1954. A similar type of work is V. Redlich (Ed.), *Moralprobleme in Umbruch der Zeit*, Munich 1957.

THE NEGATIVE APPROACH

The case for renewal in moral theology might be presented in a completely negavite way. This would consist in a direct criticism of the *Institutiones* or manuals as determining the approach and character of most writing and thinking in moral theology as well as the form and content of the seminary courses in recent centuries. And it would be possible to list in a damaging way the more obvious defects of the manuals. They have been criticized for their failure to emphasize the supernatural, Christian character of moral theology, for a tendency to reduce it to a combination of natural ethics and canon law, for their heavily legal (if not legalist) framework, and for their preoccupation with sin and their emphasis on casuistry.[2] And these criticisms have considerable justification, even if they are sometimes presented in an exaggerated way without sufficient understanding of the historical purpose and development of the manuals. Allowing for all this, the criticisms still add up to a convincing case for some renewal in moral theology.

THE UNITY-OF-THEOLOGY APPROACH

A different approach could start from the developments in other areas of theology, which because of the unity of theology must also affect moral theology. This would be a more positive and perhaps more profitable approach than the previous one.

There are many obvious connections between these other theological developments and moral theology. The biblical movement has given all theologians a new awareness of their obligation to base their thinking on the fullest understanding of the Bible available through modern scholarship. Such an increased understanding must also throw fresh light on the foundation and and practice of Christian morals. The liturgical movement and the new insights in sacramental theology highlight the community worship of the Father through Christ as central to

[2] The best known and most extreme presentation of this critical approach is J. Leclercq, *L'Enseignement de la Morale Chrêtienne*, Louvain, 1950.

Christian living and morality. All other human acts acquire their basic Christian significance from this worshipping unity with the Son. The related theology of the laity makes clear the vocation and responsibility of the individual Christian to live his life in the Church and in the world as a member and witness of Christ. The implications of the ecumenical movement for Catholic theology will only gradually be realized. But already, and even in moral theology, the efforts to explain oneself to Christians who are without any strong legal or Aristotelian tradition in morals, and the meeting with a morality couched in more personal terms, have had enriching results. In general the renewed theology of the Church and of the Christian in the world has considerable importance for the behaviour of Christians and for the theology that deals with it, namely, Christian moral theology.

FROM THE NATURE AND STRUCTURE OF CHRISTIAN MORAL THEOLOGY

A more profound and satisfying method of approach would be to examine the nature and structure of Christian moral theology and see what properties should characterize it. In this way it will be possible to judge how far the conventional presentation of the manuals is in need of renewal. The criticisms of the first approach will appear in their true context without the same danger of exaggeration, while the influences of other theological developments will be given cohesion and unity.

Morality concerns men's behaviour. Christian morality concerns how men called to be Christians should behave and live. The theology of Christian morality then is a theology of Christian life. It investigates and presents in scientific, organized fashion, the way of life revealed by God in Christ. It studies Christ and the Christian revelation as a way of life.[3] From the basic structure of this way of life made known in Christ it is possible to derive the characteristic properties of Christian moral theology.

[3] 'I am the way, the truth and the life,' *John* 14: 6.

The distinction between dogmatic and moral theology is a relatively late development, which, for all its usefulness for study purposes, has tended to obscure the unity of theology as the one scientific study of God's revelation of himself to man. It is tempting to describe dogmatic theology as the study of this revelation as a system of truth, and moral theology as the study of it as a way of life.[4] But the truth is the life. And the distinction is artificial, whereby dogmatic theology stops short of presenting the truth as life, allowing moral theology to deal with the immediate life-giving consequences of this truth, how it affects man's life and behaviour. It is therefore sometimes difficult to decide whether to treat a particular section of theology (for example, grace) in dogma or moral. Where one actually draws the line of division is of less importance than the insistence on the unity of theology and on the fact that the truths of the Christian faith form the springs of Christian life. So the truths elaborated in dogmatic theology must be examined as sources of life in moral theology.

This can be expressed in a slightly different manner. Theology by definition is basically about God, for us the God of Revelation, God as he has revealed or communicated himself to man. This communication took the form of a series of interventions in human history. All earlier interventions were preparatory to and derive their meaning from God's supreme communication of himself to man, in the incarnation, death and resurrection of his Son. Christian theology studies Christ as the primary manifestation of the divine to man and all other manifestations in the light of Christ. But this communication or manifestation of himself to man by God was at the same time an invitation to man to respond by giving himself to God and so sharing divine life. Man's self-giving and sharing like God's self-manifesting and inviting are achieved in Christ. And this whole complex reality forms the subject-matter of Christian theology. Moral

[4] For a comprehensive account of the different approaches to this problem cf. R. Hofmann, *Moraltheologische Erkenntnis- und Methodenlehre*, Munich, 1963.

theology concentrates on man's response to God in Christ through his life and behaviour, but it must study it in terms of invitation-response because it is a response to a definite invitation.[5]

The life of the Christian is organized or structured in this way about these focal points—God communicating himself to man as an invitation in Christ and man responding in Christ to God. And moral theology, if it is to be true to the lines of the reality which it studies, must allow this inner structure to stand out clearly in its scientific presentation of the life and behaviour demanded of man in the Christian revelation. This will not be achieved by a brief introductory paragraph, or even chapter, on this structure in outlining the general principles of moral theology. The general principles must be seen as built into this structure and each special section of moral theology should be discussed in terms of God's invitation through Christ to man in this particular area and man's response again through Christ. And it is from this invitation-response relationship between God and man founded in Christ that the properties of a scientific presentation of Christian moral theology may be derived.

1 *God-centred*

God, not man, and certainly not any impersonal institution like the law, should be at the centre of moral theology. It is through his giving himself to God that man attains perfection. But the perfection of man should not appear as the primary and guiding principle in presenting moral theology. This perfection is important and a necessary consequence of the Christian life but it is not of first importance. It can be maintained that ontologically man's perfection implies the love and service of God and his glory. But it is the way of implication that is objectionable—with its appearance of a subordination of God to man's satisfaction. It is to those who first of all seek the kingship of God, who give themselves unconditionally to him in response to the invitation

[5] Cf. Neuhäusler, *Anspruch und Antwort Gottes*, Düsseldorf, 1962.

he issues in Christ, that all other things (man's complete perfection) will be added.[6] And the most enlightened self-seeking is no substitute for God-seeking.

The search for self-perfection as the principle of morality easily issues in exaggerated emphasis on the law and the works of the law as a tangible assurance of perfection—the very attitude Christ came to condemn.[7] The true meaning of the divine (and human) law is obscured. It tends to be regarded as self-explanatory instead of being understood as a necessary guide in reading the divine invitation in any given situation. It is only within the limits of divine law that man can truly respond to God. But the observance of particular laws is no substitute for and no guarantee of this loving response. Unless a man responds to God out of love, the fulfilment of law will profit him nothing.[8]

2 *Based on Christ*

The mediating link in the structure of Christian living and so of Christian moral theology is Christ. It is in and through Christ that God has issued his invitation to man, and it is only in and through Christ that man can accept and respond to this invitation.[9] A proper appreciation of God whom man seeks, in his unity and trinity, in his activity in the world, in his invitation to man to share his life and his gift to man of the power to understand and accept the invitation, depends on an ever-deepening understanding of the divine self-disclosure in Christ. The role of the person Christ, God become man, God communicating himself to man at the supreme level and man in utter response to God, should dominate any scientific account of moral theology, any account that organizes moral theology about its central truths. And it must shape the general outline as well as each individual section of moral theology.

[6] *Matt.* 6: 33; *Luke* 12: 31.
[7] *Luke* 18: 10 ff.; *Matt.* 21: 31. Cf. *Gal.* 2: 16, 21; 3: 10.
[8] 1 *Cor.* 13.
[9] Cf. *John* 14: 6 ff. etc.

Recent attempts at renewal in moral theology have illustrated the need and effectiveness of this approach. The pioneer work of exegete and moral theologian Fritz Tillmann [10] was centred on the evangelical idea of the imitation and following of Christ (*die Nachfolge Christi*) as the determining principle of moral theology. Emile Mersch, S.J., had a similar inspiration for his *Morale et Corps Mystique*.[11] And the most influential single work in the whole task of renewing moral theology, that of Bernhard Häring, C.SS.R., was simply called *The Law of Christ* [12] (*das Gesetz Christi*) and placed great emphasis on the invitation-response structure in Christ as its cardinal idea.

The position of Christ as the corner-stone on which the Christian life and moral theology must be erected will be expounded more fully in Father Fuchs's lecture.[13] Here it is sufficient to derive from it two subsidiary properties which should characterize the moral theologian's thinking and writing. Christ as the basis of Christian life is present to man today in the Church. And here he is encountered in two primary and divinely-given forms, word and sacrament. In the word of God as recorded under divine inspiration in the Bible and in the sacraments instituted by him as effective signs of grace in the Church, the Christian and the theologian find their most immediate contact with Christ and Christian life. To be true to its Christian character, moral theology must be biblical and sacramental.

(a) *Biblical*

All Christian theology must be biblical, based on the divine account of Christ, of the preparation for his coming and of his life and teaching. No other source of theology can compare with

[10] F. Tillmann, *Handbuch der Katholischen Sittenlehre; Bd. III Die Idee der Nachfolge Christi; Bd. IV Die Verwirklichung der Nachfolge Christi.* Düsseldorf, 1933 (4th ed. 1952). A summary of his ideas may be found in his single volume work, *The Master Calls*, London, 1962. Cf. Schulz, *Nachfolgen und Nachahmen*, Munich, 1962.

[11] 3rd ed. Brussels, 1949.

[2] In English translation Vols. I, II. Cork, 1961, 1963.

[3] *The Law of Christ* p. 70.

the Bible. It must of course be studied in the Church of Christ, faithful to his guidance of the Church, but it must be studied, constantly invoked and referred to in all attempts to develop theology. The Bible is obviously not a theology text-book. And reading the Bible is not a substitute for theology. What is called biblical theology, the systematic study of the truths of the Bible in the context and terms of the Bible, is not what we understand by a developed Christian theology. A developed theology takes account of all the available sources of knowledge about God and man, and of the world and the civilization in which Christ's message must be preached and lived. But the Bible as the word of God is necessary reading for all literate Christians. For the professional teachers of the Christian message a scientific understanding of the Bible is indispensable. Today understanding of the Bible has increased considerably. In its growth and composition, in its gradual manifestation of God to man, in the dominant ideas which that manifestation reveals and the immediate contact with the person of Christ which it gives, the Bible must dominate the moral theologian's thinking, if he is to present Christ and his message as a way of life.

Referring the reader to a dogmatic tract for anything more than can be derived from natural ethics or expressed in a legal framework, invocation of isolated texts on a particular virtue or sin, do not suffice to make a moral theology text-book biblical. And it seems hardly unfair to criticize the manuals of recent vintage as lacking in this biblical character.

(b) *Sacramental*

As a theology of the Christian's living and behaviour, moral theology must be sacramental. The sacraments are at once signs and sources of man's sharing the life of Christ himself. Performed in the Church, they are events of real significance in which the Christian encounters Christ. In their different ways they form the high points of God's communicating himself to the man responsive in Christ. By this sacramental communication man is assimilated to Christ and united with him in all his activity.

This activity becomes Christian activity, Christ-activity, expressing the Christ-life which man now enjoys and which demands expression in his every act.

The sacramental source of Christian life and activity emphasizes its character as a divine gift.[14] We have nothing that we have not received.[15] Of ourselves we can do nothing. It is only as branches of the true vine that we can bear fruit.[16] The true, Christian and gratuitous character of every one of our good actions, thus revealed, will not tolerate any impression of self-justification through the observance of laws. Such moralism is not Christian morality.

As man's union with the Son in the worship of the Father is the apex of his vocation, so the eucharistic liturgy, as the fullest realization of that in the pilgrim days of the Church,[17] assumes its rightful place at the centre of Christian living, in which every human act is an act of worship, giving glory to the Father through the Son. The liturgical renewal will remain the preserve of the esthete or *élite* unless consciousness of the worshipping character of his every act is awakened in the Christian.

This human act of his has a further sacramental value. It bears witness before the whole world to the life that is in him. It is the sign of Christ's grace at work in the world, especially for those for whom the Church's sacramental rites are not yet signs of faith. Elaboration of this witness or sign-value of the Christian's human act gives a new dimension to life and morality. And it provides a remarkable antidote to the legalism and minimalism sometimes found in Catholic presentations of morality and frequently a source of scandal to Catholics themselves and other Christians. To manifest the full implications of the sacramental character of Christian life and activity in every sphere is one of the tasks of a renewed moral theology.

[14] *John* 1: 16; *Rom.* 1: 5, etc.
[15] 2 *Cor.* 3: 5; *Gal.* 1: 12.
[16] *John* 15: 4-5.
[7] Const. De Sacra Liturgia, § 2.

3 *Personal to Man*

As the study of man's activity in responding to God's invitation, moral theology should be presented in a way that takes account of man's dignity as a person. The third focal point in the structure of moral theology, man, may never be treated as an object or as an impersonal source of material actions, the morality of which are judged independently of the person performing them. The human response which these actions express is as personal as the divine invitation which prompts them. In the moral theology which studies and judges them, this personal character should emerge very clearly.

The personal quality of Christian morality is very evident in the biblical writings on which it is based. The appeal of Christ called for man's μετάνοια, complete personal turning to God.[18] The acceptance of God's final communication of himself in Christ involves total personal commitment. God in Christ does not ask for the lip-service of those who say Lord, Lord.[19] He cannot be satisfied with those who honour him with their lips while their hearts are far from him.[20] The external observance of laws, even the physical offering of sacrifices by those who have refused this personal self-giving, is of no account.[21] It is what comes forth from a man's heart that is of value for man and to God.[22] The whole law of morality, of the human response which God demands, is summed up in the total gift of self through love.[23] And this love must exceed all human ties and be prepared to follow in Christ's way of the Cross even unto death.[24]

Conversion through personal commitment to God in Christ is the beginning of Christian life for each man. But it is a response which has to be renewed and deepened every day. Conversion

[18] *Mark* 1: 15, par.
[19] *Matt.* 7: 31.
[20] *Is.* 29: 13; *Matt.* 15: 7-9.
[21] *Mark* 12: 33; *Matt.* 9: 13; 1 *Sam.* 15: 27; *Hos.* 6: 6.
[22] *Matt.* 12: 34 f.; *Luke* 6: 45.
[23] *Mark* 12: 28–34, par.
[24] *Matt.* 10: 34–9, par.

is a permanent demand in the life of the Christian. Daily he must take up his cross, accept the challenge of the moment and follow Christ.[25] In every situation in which he can accept or reject, each human act will express this acceptance (generously or weakly) or it will reject it. And face to face with this decision, the Christian is not alone. Through his union with Christ, he enjoys the guidance and strength of the Spirit of Christ [26] who has been poured forth in his heart.[27] In fulfilling the highest demands of his personality by responding positively to the divine call in each situation, he is allowing the Spirit who has been given to him to act through him. The life and grace of Christ which is his, finds its expression in his personal action.

The biblical stress on the personal quality which moral theology should have, is confirmed by many of the philosophical and psychological developments of today. The deeper understanding of the individual human person and of his particular situation, activity and vocation, to which various modern philosophical movements have drawn attention, is extremely valuable to moral theology. The insistence of the personalist movement for instance on the supreme value and dignity of the person, who may never be treated as a mere functionary, still less as an object or thing, harmonizes with and enriches a theology of invitation-response, while it is quite alien to a purely legalist system of morality. Similarly the existentialist movement, for all its deviations and distortions precisely in the field of morality, has given the (moral) theologian an increased awareness of the importance of the concrete, individual man existing in all his uniqueness as this particular man in this particular situation. And the growth of value-philosophy enabled theologians to present moral realities in a way that was truer to the full moral reality, for example, of justice or chastity, and less dependent on legal expression. It is significant that the successors to Tillmann, in his attempt at a purely biblical renewal of the theology, have

[25] *Luke* 9: 23, par.
[26] Cf. *Rom.* 8.
[27] *Gal.* 4: 6; *Rom.* 8: 15; 2 *Cor.* 1: 22.

tried to integrate the positive elements of these philosophical movements into their work. This is clear in the work of the influential professional moralists like Häring,[28] Gilleman [29] and Fuchs.[30] It is even truer of Karl Rahner [31] whose work has been the most searching dialogue yet composed between modern man and the Christian message, and who, while he may be professionally described as a dogmatic theologian, is one of the most fertile influences today in moral as in all Catholic theology.

These insights of the philosophers existed in some degree already in theology, even if they had been largely ignored or undeveloped. But the radical developments of modern psychology from Freud to the present day, revealing new and unsuspected regions in man's personality, present a new challenge particularly to the theology of man's personal activity. The ideas and discoveries are still incomplete, still the subject of great controversy; but at the practical and therapeutic level we have an immediate impression of the importance of personal maturity through the recognition and acceptance of oneself, one's gifts and limitations, and through growth in the capacity to love as the highest personal act.

Psychological health and maturity free man from certain irrational forces or rather enable him to harness his sub-rational forces and to give himself in love to God and his fellowman in a fuller way. Any developments in knowledge and technique which help man to grow in this way, are welcome additions to the moral theologian's picture of the human person responding to God. While he must take account of the emotional and other forces which inhibit man's freedom and so reduce his responsibility, he is primarily interested in the advances of psychology

[28] Vide supra note 12.

[29] G. Gillemann, *The Primacy of Charity in Moral Theology*, London, 1959.

[30] J. Fuchs, *Theologia Moralis Generalis*, Rome, 1963.

[31] Rahner's relevant works are scattered through his articles and the various collections of them. Some of those most directly concerned with moral theology may be found in translation in *Nature and Grace*, London, 1963; *Mission and Grace* I, II, London, 1963, 1964; and *The Dynamic Element in the Church*, London, 1964

or psychiatry, not as providing excusing causes or impediments to voluntariety, but as providing help to each man in attaining the fullest measure of maturity and freedom possible to him, and so making that complete personal response in Christ to which God is calling him. The integration of the established conclusions of modern psychology into moral theology is a task that demands a very personal presentation of the Christian message. A predominantly legal presentation will be unequal to it. It is only in a moral theology that is true to the personal and living character of Christian morals as derived from Christ and the New Testament, that the psychological and philosophical concepts of today can find their real home. The place of the legal precept or prohibition may never be ignored, but it cannot express the full reality or be given first place in the moral theology of a Christian person.

(a) *Positive*

As a theology of personal response to an invitation, moral theology should be presented in positive terms. God does not invite man to no-thing, to not-do things, to avoid things. He invites man to a personal love of himself. This love man manifests by responding to the manifestations of the divine which, summed up in Christ, are now mediated to man through word and sacrament and Christian moral values. In seeking the moral values of, for example, truth or justice or chastity inherent in any situation with which he is faced, man is responding in love to the God whom they reflect and mediate. It is from the supreme value, the *summum bonum* which is God, that these intermediate perfections or values, really the objects of the Christian virtues, derive their goodness for man. In seeing them as reflections of the divine, man expresses his loving response to God and perfects himself by increasing in himself the image of God and likeness to Christ.

The true Christian significance of these values has been frequently diminished in the legalist framework of moral theology and distorted by the manual preoccupation with sin or non-value.

The extent of this preoccupation may be deduced from a recent (1961) edition of a standard and in general comparatively balanced manual of moral theology.

The half-volume entitled *De Sexto et Nono Praeceptis* contains more than sixty-five pages and deals with four questions. After an introductory paragraph, quoting the sixth and ninth commandments from the Book of Exodus, *Quaestio I* dealing very properly with the virtue and headed *De castitate et pudicitia*, begins on p. 8 and runs to p. 10; *Quaestio II* headed *De luxuria in genere*, runs from p. 11 to p. 20; *Quaestio III De peccatis luxuriae consummatis*, pp. 21–43 (including an appendix *De sexualitate abnormi*), and *Quaestio IV De peccatis luxuriae non consummatis*, pp. 43–58, complete the theological treatment of chastity. Three questions on the vice, comprising forty-eight pages, are balanced by one question on the virtue comprising three pages, of which almost one page is taken up with the question *Quomodo virginitas amittatur*. No matter how excellent the opening two pages on the virtue might be, they could scarcely counterbalance the other almost fifty pages dealing with the vice or sins against the virtue. And this predominantly negative treatment has not been confined to the virtue of chastity, although it was here that it may have been most harmful.

In defence of such treatment it is sometimes alleged that the purpose of the manuals is the training of confessors. This defence is not altogether convincing. The manual itself claims to be a text-book of moral theology and should be criticized as such. In particular there is no comparable positive treatment of chastity at a theological level to which the seminarian may turn in his course. And even as a guide for confessors the predominantly negative treatment is inadequate. Sin is a negation, and the negative has meaning only in relation to the positive. Sin in general must be described as man's personal rejection of God as he communicates himself to man. This communication may be perceived only in a general, unreflecting, implicit way. But there must be some such implicit understanding of God and his summons to a particular act, before you can have the rejection of God which sin always involves.

God himself has revealed how this communication of himself is implied in each good act to which man is obliged. It is the business of the moral theologian to make as explicit as possible in each area of human activity the implicit divine invitation, by clarifying the positive value involved as it reflects the divine goodness and becomes a suitable term of man's act of loving God. In sex as in every other area of human activity moral theology seeks to understand how God manifests himself and how man may recognize and respond to that manifestation. It is the rejection of the divine invitation enshrined in chastity or of the reflection of God in sex, that is the sin of unchastity. But the meaning and malice of unchastity can be understood only in so far as chastity is understood. The negative as always derives its meaning from the positive it denies. This has always been assumed in our teaching of morality. The principles of morality were first of all statements of the obligatory values proposed to us by God and the Church in each sphere of our activity. But this became obscured in the elaboration of the legal and negative expression of the limits within which these values could be realized. To train priests in the discernment of sins of unchastity or any other sins the primary requirement is a full study of the virtue itself. As a preacher as well as a confessor this positive understanding of the riches of the divine invitation in each area of Christian living, will be indispensable to the priest.

(b) *Dynamic*

In attempting to present a programme of living, moral theology must reveal the dynamism of life. Life is a process of growth and development. It has an inner dynamism. The Christian life as a personal response to God has a dynamism also. It is a going somewhere, not just staying somewhere. It is dynamic, not static. A Christian is either going forward, however gradually, towards God or backwards away from him into sin. A static theology distorts the reality by ignoring this movement and presenting the Christian as staying somewhere, out of sin, within the law or vice versa. It tends to become preoccupied with the limits dividing sin and non-sin, while its attention is distracted from the central reality, God in Christ, who gives the limits their meaning and whom man should be seeking. In this way it can create insoluble problems for people who may become obsessed with the limits beyond which lie the sins they know they should but feel they cannot avoid, while they never turn their eyes to the merciful God who is calling them and to whom they will come a step at a time.

(c) *In community*

Finally the personal character of moral theology implies that it should have a community or social aspect also. A person is not an isolated individual. By birth and baptism he belongs to society or community. He is bound to other persons by multiple ties of blood and dependence and common destiny. All these ties find a deeper significance in Christianity. As Christ was raised up to draw all men to him,[32] all men are bound more closely together under their new head, with whom they should form one body.[33] In man's response to God's invitation in Christ, the community context must colour his every action. This was long ago proclaimed by Christ himself in summarizing the response under love of God and the neighbour,[34] and its implications spelled out by St John, as he denied the possibility of loving God without loving one's brother.[35]

At the human level the corporate destiny of mankind was never more intensely felt than it is today. This destiny is ultimately a Christian one. And it makes it all the more necessary that commitment to the community should be evident in every section of Christian moral theology, so that no suspicion of a spiritual or material self-centred individualistic attitude may colour our moral teaching.

[32] *John* 3: 16.
[33] 1 *Cor.* 11: 3; 12: 12, etc.
[34] *Mark* 12: 28–34, par. *John* 13: 34 ff.
[35] 1 *John* 4: 7 ff.

CONCLUSION

The central mystery of Christianity is the expression of the one God in three divine persons. It is through their roles in his salvation that they are revealed to man. The Father out of mercy for man in his sinful helplessness initiates the plan of human salvation which is accomplished in the sending of the Son. The radical salvation or reconciliation of man with the Father is extended to the individual man by the giving of the Holy Spirit to Christ's Church. In the salvation of the race then, as well as in the salvation of the individual human person, the Father communicates himself to man and realizes his plan for man in the Son. Man responds to the Father in the Son through the power and guidance of the Spirit. It is with the understanding of and co-operation with this activity of the three divine persons in the world and in each person, that Christian moral theology is concerned.[36] It is to enable man both to understand and co-operate more fully, that the present efforts at renewal are directed. By respecting the structure of moral theology and its characteristics as indicated here, renewal may be profitably attempted.

[36] Cf. Spicq, *St Paul and Christian Living*, Dublin, 1964.

THE LAW,
THE PROPHETS AND THE GOSPEL

Wilfrid Harrington, O.P.

It is still too readily taken for granted that the legalistic religion of pharisaism, so severely criticized by our Lord, is a fair enough picture of Old Testament religion and morality—a way of life all hedged about by futile and soul-destroying laws. The truth of the matter is that, until the later stages of Judaism, the Torah was not at all regarded as an oppressive burden but was gladly accepted as God's gift to his people. Jesus did not reproach the scribes and pharisees for their attachment to the law but for their failure to grasp the spirit of it; immersed in their casuistry they had neglected the 'weightier matters of the law, justice and mercy and faith.' [1] Indeed, the pharisaic outlook is more in harmony with bare and bald casuistic teaching than it is representative of biblical moral doctrine. The renewal of our moral theology can be forwarded by a study of the Old Testament as well as of the New.

The object of this paper is to indicate something of the depth and breadth of the Torah, the will of God for his people, and to trace its pervasive influence through the life and literature of Israel. It will be shown that the moral teaching of the prophets developed in harmony with the law and that there is no conflict between prophet and priest. Finally it will be seen that Christ brought a new dimension into human life and that ever since the moral life of the Christian is, or ought to be, guided by the law of Christ—a commandment of love.

[1] *Matt.* 23:23.

I THE LAW

The Hebrew word *torah* has a wider signification, one less strictly juridical, than the *nomos* of the LXX or the English 'law'; it is a 'teaching' given by God to men in order to regulate their conduct. That is why the whole Pentateuch, and not only the legislation, is called the Torah. In fact, framed in a narrative setting, the Pentateuch contains the ensemble of prescriptions which ruled the moral, social and religious life of the people. All of these prescriptions, moral, juridical and cultic, have a religious character, and the whole corpus is presented as the charter of a covenant with Yahweh and is linked with the narrative of happenings in the desert where the covenant was made.

While it remains true that the basis of the legislation goes back to the time of Moses, the Pentateuch, in its present form, includes many laws of later ages. It is simply not conceivable that a legal code, drawn up for a small nomad people in the thirteenth century B.C., would have remained unchanged for over a thousand years while that people became successively an agricultural community, a monarchy and a church. Laws are made to be applied and must necessarily be adapted to changing conditions. So, for instance, much of the priestly legislation found in *Exod.* 25–31, 35–40 bears the stamp of later times. The Covenant Code [2] is the law of a pastoral and agricultural society, and it met the conditions of Israel already settled in Palestine. The ritual laws of *Exod.* 34: 14–26 date from the same time but show some influence of Deuteronomy. Leviticus took its final shape after the Exile, in the Second Temple, but the basis of it goes back to the primitive ritual of the desert. The Law of Holiness [3] seems to have been codified towards the close of the monarchy. The deuteronomical code [4] is earlier than the fall of Samaria in 721, and though it shows a development that is influenced by an appreciation of the love of Yahweh for his

[2] *Exod.* 20–23.
[3] *Levit.* 17–26.
[4] *Deut.* 12–26.

people and of Israel's consequent obligation to act as he would act, it is basically a re-interpretation and a new presentation of earlier laws.

It seems possible to identify some of the earlier laws of the Pentateuch on the basis of form. Two general types are readily noted: casuistic (or hypothetical) law and apodeictic (or categorical) law. Both types are well represented in *Exod.* 22; the hypothetical type in vv 1–17 (' If . . . ', with the provision in the third person) and the apodeictic form in vv 18, 21 f. (' Thou shalt not . . . ', with the injunction in the second person). Hypothetical law was common throughout the ancient world, especially in Mesopotamia and among the Hittites, and is best represented in the Code of Hammurabi.[5] Apodeictic law is peculiar to Israel. This fact powerfully strengthens the argument that the Decalogue (to take a striking example) goes back to Moses. The Ten Commandments, in Hebrew the ' Ten Words,' are given twice; [6] both versions are in apodeictic form—though several of the commandments have been expanded in later times—and both go back to a common primitive form set out in sharp, terse language. In general, it may be said that the apodeictic laws are early and may well represent a nucleus that originated with Moses. However, for our purpose, instead of analysing and comparing the various codes within the Pentateuch, it is more profitable to set that work in its covenant background and to examine the four great strands of which it is woven.

The Covenant

To express the nature of the link which exists between God and his people the Old Testament uses the word *berith* (rendered in the Greek by *diathēkē* and in Latin by *testamentum*). In English it is generally translated ' covenant.' This term covenant, which in its technical theological sense concerns the relations of man with God, was borrowed from the social experience of men, from the fact of treaties and alliances between peoples and

[5] Cf. J. B. Pritchard, *Ancient Near-Eastern Texts*, Princeton, 1955, 163–80.
[6] *Exod.* 20: 2–17; *Deut.* 5: 6–18.

individuals. In practice, the religious use of the term regards a special type of covenant, that in which one partner takes the initiative and imposes the conditions. This is exactly the pattern of the Sinai covenant.

At Sinai the people, delivered from Egyptian bondage, entered into a covenant with Yahweh and the cult of Yahweh was established as the national religion. A study of Hittite treaties has shed light on the nature of this covenant.[7] Two types of treaty may be distinguished: the parity pact and the suzerainty pact. In a parity covenant both partners, standing on equal terms, bound themselves by bilateral obligations. The suzerainty covenant, on the other hand, was made between a king and his vassal and was unilateral. The suzerain 'gave' a covenant and the vassal was obliged to accept and obey the conditions of the suzerain. Yet such a covenant was not just an assertion of power and authority on the part of the suzerain; it was explicitly regarded and presented as an act of benevolence, and the vassal accepted the obligations in a sense of gratitude. In keeping with this conception the covenant was couched in an 'I-Thou' dialogue form.

At the vision of the burning bush Yahweh revealed to Moses both his name and his plan for Israel; he willed to deliver Israel from Egypt and to instal his people in the land of Canaan.[8] This plan presupposed that Israel was the object of his choice and the recipient of a promise; the Exodus demonstrated that God was capable of imposing his will ('You have seen how I bore you on eagles' wings and brought you to myself'—*Exod.* 19: 4) and the people responded by faith.[9] Then God revealed the terms of the covenant: 'If you will obey my voice and keep my covenant, you shall be my own possession among all peoples; for all the earth is mine, and you shall be to me a kingdom of priests and a holy nation.'[10] Israel will henceforth be his kingdom, his

[7] G. E. Mendenhall, 'Law and Covenant in Israel and the Ancient Near East,' *The Biblical Archaeologist*, 17 (1954), 26–76.

[8] *Exod.* 3: 7–10.

[9] *Ibid.* 14: 31.

[10] *Ibid.* 19: 5 f.

people will render him due cult. In return, God will 'tabernacle' in the midst of his people: 'They shall know that I am the Lord their God, who brought them forth out of the land of Egypt that I might dwell among them.' [11] The Sinai covenant, however, was conditional. In granting this covenant to Israel and in making promises God imposed conditions which Israel must observe. But these laws and institutions were laid down and established in order that Israel should be a holy people; they are an expression of divine benevolence, even though failure to observe them will entail a curse.[12]

The covenant of Sinai revealed in a definitive manner an essential aspect of the plan of salvation. God had willed to join himself to men by establishing a cultic community dedicated to his service, ruled by his law, the recipient of his promises; the New Testament will fully realize this divine project. Although the covenant was God's free gift to Israel it became enmeshed in the historical destiny of Israel to such an extent that salvation tended to be regarded as the reward of human fidelity to the law. Its limitation to one nation tended to obscure the universal scope of God's plan, while the promises of temporal rewards could cause men to lose sight of the religious object of the covenant —the establishment of the kingship of God over Israel and through Israel over the whole world.[13] Nonetheless, the covenant of Sinai dominated Israel's history and the development of revelation. It is the inspiration of the Torah.

The Yahwist [14]

The work of the Yahwist is a synthesis, both in form and in substance, and yet this writer is one of the most creative literary artists of Israel. He gathered together the traditions of the tribes

[11] *Ibid.* 29: 46. [12] *Levit.* 26: 14–39.

[13] J. Giblet-P. Grelot, *Vocabulaire de Théologie Biblique* (ed. Léon-Dufour), Paris, 1962, 21.

[14] The earliest of the four traditions which make up the Pentateuch is named the *Yahwistic*; it is of Judean origin and took its final form in the tenth century B.C. The *Elohistic* tradition developed in Israel and was fixed in the ninth century. The

and of the sanctuaries and reworked them in order to make the old relevant to the new. Many of these old narratives are aetiologies, that is, their purpose was to explain, in a popular way, some facts in tribal history, or the names of places, or certain aspects of the cult. The Yahwist combined these different materials in a new literary structure, a great epic extending from the creation of the world to the conquest of Transjordan. Some of the individual stories taken by themselves, for example, the angel marriages [15] and the Tower of Babel [16] betray a primitive theological outlook; but, as used by the Yahwist, they play their part in the presentation of his elevated theology.

The Yahwist is keenly aware of the forces of evil at work in the world; he has no illusions about humanity and he unpityingly exposes human weakness, but he is an optimist at heart. He has confidence in nature and her laws which will not be disrupted by another deluge. He shows the persistence and expansion of life, the good fortune of the sons of Jacob, Israel delivered from slavery, the twelve tribes on their way to a land flowing with milk and honey. This optimism is based on a knowledge of Yahweh, on confidence in his plan and in his power. Yahweh is transcendent but draws near to men, and this nearness is expressed in bold anthropomorphisms. God demands of men faith, courage and confidence in the traditions and in the life of the nation.[17]

Deuteronomical tradition is confined to the Book of Deuteronomy. The nucleus of it was formed in Israel before 721 B.C.; it was promulgated in Judah during the reform of Josiah (640–609) and an enlarged edition of it was prepared during the Exile (586–538). The *Priestly* tradition is particularly interested in the organization of the sanctuary, in the sacrifices and in the sacred personnel. It developed during the Exile and took its final shape after the return. The priests, who were responsible for fixing this tradition, also gave its definitive form to the whole Pentateuch. We may say briefly that Genesis, Exodus and Numbers are a combination of the yahwistic, elohistic and priestly traditions; Leviticus has the priestly tradition only, and the deuteronomical tradition is found in Deuteronomy alone.

[15] *Gen.* 6: 1–4. [16] *Ibid.* 11: 1–9.

[17] H. Cazelles, *Introduction à la Bible I* (ed. A. Robert A. Feuillet), Tournai, 1957, 348–80.

The Yahwist's epic falls into three parts: primeval history, the patriarchal tradition, the Mosaic tradition. The primeval history, constructed from elements of very different kinds, proclaims that all evil comes from sin and testifies to a growth in evil. Yet the widening chasm between God and man remains spanned by a bridge of mercy and is matched by an increasing power of grace. In the call of Abraham [18] primeval history is linked with sacred history and finds its meaning in this link.[19] The Yahwist continues his theological synthesis by utilizing the patriarchal traditions. In his eyes Abraham is the model patriarch, yet the promises of God are destined not for him but for his posterity. Right through the patriarchal epoch run the cult of the same God (the ' God of the fathers ') and the participation of successive generations in the same divine promises. Similarly, the God who revealed himself to Moses at the burning bush is the ' God of the fathers '[20] and it is Moses who communicated to the people the will of God, his words, in the form of a ritual decalogue.[21]

The Elohist

The Elohist begins with the call of Abraham and so does not have a primeval history; in this he lacks the scope of the Yahwist. Similarly, the Elohist does not show the theological depth, much less the literary artistry, of the Yahwist. Yet what he loses in vividness and brilliance he gains somewhat in moral sensibility. His sense of sin is more refined than that of the Yahwist. So, for instance, he avoids the impression that Abraham had lied to Abimelech by stating explicitly that Sarah was the patriarch's half-sister.[22] For him the law is more moral than cultic. The basis of it, as it finds expression in the Decalogue, concerns man's duties towards God and towards his neighbour. These duties are made more explicit in the Covenant Code [23] where the

[18] *Gen.* 12: 1–3.
[19] G. von Rad, *Genesis*, London 1961, 23, 148–50.
[20] *Exod.* 3: 16.
[21] *Ibid.* 34: 10–28.
[22] *Gen.* 20: 12.
[23] *Exod.* 20: 22–23: 19.

respect of one's neighbour and of his goods is regulated by customs and precepts that have been sanctioned by God. The Elohist tends to emphasize the distance of God from men, at least in comparison with the Yahwist's approach. Anthropomorphism is restricted. God does not walk among men [24] but speaks from heaven [25] and in dreams.[26] Indeed it is stated explicitly: 'Let not God speak to us, lest we die.' [27] In the story of Joseph the Elohist brings out the religious significance of the events: 'As for you, you meant evil against me; but God meant it for good, to bring it about that many people should be kept alive, as they are today.' [28]

The Deuteronomist

The kernel of Deuteronomy is the legal code,[29] of northern origin, and going back ultimately to the Mosaic age; the narrative part, the three discourses of Moses, are much later, from just before and after the Exile. The second discourse [30] is especially fitting in the mouth of the great leader because the essential purpose of Deuteronomy is a revival of Mosaic teaching as it was understood in the seventh century B.C.; it is a reform programme, not an innovation. Hence the appeal for covenant renewal, made with urgency, the repetition of 'this day'—the here and now of the divine election—and the involvement of the present generation of Israel in the covenant made at Horeb.[31] The law of the one sanctuary [32] is inspired by the same reforming spirit: to preserve the purified code of Yahweh from all contamination.

[24] *Gen.* 3: 8; 18: 1 ff.
[25] *Ibid.* 21: 17.
[26] *Ibid.* 20: 3, 6; 15: 1; 18: 12.
[27] *Exod.* 20: 19.
[28] *Gen.* 50: 20.
[29] *Deut.* 12: 1; 26: 15.
[30] *Ibid.* 4: 41; 28: 64.
[31] B. W. Anderson, *The Living World of the Old Testament*, London 1958, 313.
[32] *Deut.* 12: 1–14.

In the discourses characteristic turns of phrase keep cropping up. God is always ' Yahweh thy God ' or ' Yahweh your God.' Canaan is described as ' a land flowing with milk and honey,' and, in order that they might possess it, God had delivered his people from Egypt ' with a mighty hand and an outstretched arm.' That is why the people are admonished to ' hear the voice of Yahweh your God ' and to ' keep his statutes and his commandments and ordinances ' and to ' fear Yahweh your God.' Above all, they are exhorted: ' You shall love Yahweh your God with all your heart, and with all your soul and with all your might '—the manifest influence of Hosea. And throughout there is the frequent reminder that faithful observance of the commandments of Yahweh will ensure a blessing and the warning that neglect of the commandments will bring upon them the anger of a loving but just God.

That warning should have been unnecessary for these ' statutes, commandments and ordinances ' are not a heavy burden imposed from without, but are intimate, interior: ' For this commandment which I have commanded you this day is not too hard for you; it is in your mouth and in your heart, so that you can do it.' [33] Yahweh is a Father who gives his life-giving word to Israel, the word that brings happiness and long life.

A characteristic of Deuteronomy, and one which witnesses to the northern origin of the tradition, is the influence of Hosea. Indeed, together with the whole deuteronomical history,[34] it becomes a commentary on chapter 11 of Hosea:

> When Israel was a child I loved him, and out of Egypt I called my son. But the more I called them the farther they departed from me. . . . How can I give you up, O Ephraim! [35]

[33] *Ibid.* 30: 11, 14.

[34] The books of Joshua, Judges, Samuel, Kings (with Deuteronomy as an introduction) form the deuteronomical history. The first edition of this great work was made during the reign of Josiah (640–609); the final edition was made during the Exile.

[35] *Hos.* 11: 1 f.

Hosea is not the only prophet whose influence is evident. Jeremiah [36] had foreseen a deliverance, a return, a new covenant; it was in the light of his vision that Deuteronomy was completed. And, in its final chapters too our book joins Second Isaiah who described the new journey across the desert and the victory over the nations now summoned to adore the God of Israel, the only true God. Other images are borrowed from Ezekiel who also described the return from the Exile and the new division of the holy land around the new sanctuary.[37] Thus inspired by the prophetic message Deuteronomy, in its final edition, is a witness to a crucial stage in religious history when a monarchy yielded place to a church.[38]

The Priestly Tradition

At much the same time that the deuteronomical code took shape in the north, the traditions of the Jerusalem priests were compiled in the Holiness Code.[39] Like the deuteronomical code it opens with the law of one sanctuary and then gives several series of prescriptions regarding morality, the priests, the sacrifices and the feasts; it closes like Deuteronomy with blessings and curses.[40] Israel is conceived as an '*edah*, a worshipping community, ruled by the priests. The object of the priests was to raise men to God by fidelity to the traditional laws and prescriptions. Their guiding principle was the command: 'You shall be holy; for I Yahweh your God am holy.' [41]

During the Exile the deported priests, cut off from the elaborate ritual worship of Yahweh in his Temple, saw that their duty was to organize the religious life of the community in these different surroundings and circumstances. It seemed to them that the foundations on which the religious life might be built must be a common national origin, common traditions and an authentic

[36] *Jer.* 31.
[37] *Ezek.* 37: 40–48; cf. *Deut.* 3: 12–17.
[38] H. Cazelles, *Le Deutoronome* (BJ), Paris 1958, 17.
[39] *Levit.* 17–26.
[40] *Ibid.* 26.
[41] *Ibid.* 19: 2.

priesthood. So the priestly history took shape. The religious institutions of Israel were authorized and given greater force by being set in a historical framework, and by projecting all these institutions back into the Mosaic age it was dramatically emphasized that they had their beginnings at Sinai. The whole presentation is pervaded by a theology of the divine presence and by the demands of a God of holiness.

If we look at the priestly history as a whole we see it as the fruit of a theological reflection on the ancient liturgical traditions and customs preserved by the Jerusalem priests. Fidelity to these traditions is the only guarantee of a life in union with God, the only means of bringing about the fulfilment of God's purpose for Israel. This follows from a consideration of that plan as it gradually unfolded.

> There was a covenant of God with all humanity in the person of Noah—it assured earthly existence if men would respect the life of creatures. There was a covenant with Abraham—it guaranteed his descendants a future in the promised land if they would observe the sabbath and circumcision. There was a more personal covenant with the Aaronitic priesthood which made of them the associates of God and the dispensers of the divine benefits; the cult is the sensible sign of divine grace. The monarchy had failed; in the mind of the priestly writer Aaron must henceforth take its place—Israel in exile is sustained by the priesthood in her fidelity to the national and religious traditions. For Israel is 'a kingdom (ruled by) priests and a holy nation' (*Exod.* 19: 6).[42]

The Pentateuch

The religion of the Old Testament, like that of the New, is a historical religion; it is based on the revelation made by God to certain men in given places and on the interventions of God at certain determined moments. The Pentateuch, which traces the history of these relations of God with the world, is the foundation

[42] H. Cazelles, *Introduction à la Bible I*, 376.

of the Jewish religion, its sacred book *par excellence*, its law. In it the Israelite found the explanation of his destiny and a way of life.

The Pentateuch is drawn into a unity by the threads of promise and election, of covenant and law which run through it. To Adam and Eve, after the Fall, God gives the assurance of salvation in the distant future; after the Flood he reassures Noah that the earth will never again be so disastrously stricken. Abraham is the man of promises: for himself and for his posterity and through them for all mankind. In God's free choice of Abraham the election of Israel is foreseen and included. The Pentateuch is also the book of covenants: tacit with Adam, explicit with Noah, Abraham and Moses. Each covenant is a free exercise of divine initiative, an act of benevolence; God demands in return fidelity and obedience. The law which he gives will make explicit the divine demands and prepare the way for the fulfilment of the promises. The unifying themes of the Pentateuch continue into the rest of the Old Testament, for the Pentateuch is not complete in itself. It tells of the promise but not of its fulfilment, and it closes before the entry into the promised land. But even when the Conquest is achieved the fulfilment is not yet, for the promise looks ultimately to Christ, to the new covenant and to his commandment.

2 THE PROPHETS

Though in its earliest forms prophetism in Israel was little different from the same phenomenon in Mesopotamia, and especially in Phoenicia and Canaan, it developed into something distinctive, into something unique in fact, and became one of the most significant factors in the history of the chosen people. Indeed the prophetic movement, by itself, goes far to explain the survival of the Jewish nation. But the prophets did more than assure the survival of a people. They carried on a religious tradition which they had inherited, fostered its development between the eighth and fourth centuries, and passed it on, immeasurably enriched, to Judaism. They were entirely faithful to the dogma fixed in the Mosaic age, ethical monotheism,[43] and exploited it to the full. They were guides, carefully chosen—specially raised—along a vital and precarious stage of the spiritual journey that led to Christ. Here we shall be content to sketch the moral doctrine of some of the greatest of them.

Amos, the earliest of the ' writing ' prophets, is the champion of justice. He took his stand on the essential justice of God and vindicated the moral order established by God and enshrined in his Covenant. So he mercilessly castigated the disorders that prevailed in an era of hectic prosperity. To his eyes the symptoms of social decay were glaring: wealth, concentrated in the hands of a few—the leaders of the people—had corrupted its possessors; oppression of the poor was rife; the richly endowed national religion with its elaborate ceremonial provided a comfortable atmosphere of self-righteousness. 'The ordinary Israelite, we may be sure, felt that he had the privilege of belonging to an uncommonly religious nation, which was properly rewarded for its piety by this unwonted prosperity.' [44] It is this dangerous complacency that the prophets set out to shatter.

The series of oracles [45] shows how dramatically he could accomplish his task. The people listened, doubtless with approval, to the threatened punishment of God on six neighbouring nations. Then comes the climax, the seventh oracle (the oracle against Judah—*Amos* 2: 4 f.—is a later addition) and, out of the blue, the prophet's thunderbolt strikes Israel! Yahweh is clearly shown to be the master of all peoples,[46] but he has chosen one people: the whole family which he brought up out of Egypt.[47] With the privilege of that choice goes a corresponding obligation: ' You only have I known of all the families of the earth, therefore I will punish you for all your iniquities.' [48] Israel has received more and of her more will be required; divine justice demands it.

[43] Ethical monotheism: belief in one God who imposes a moral order; the one God of Israel is a just God who demands of his people obedience to his righteous law.
[44] C. H. Dodd, *The Bible Today*, Cambridge 1961, 39.
[45] *Amos* 1: 2–2: 16.
[46] *Ibid.* 9: 7. [47] *Ibid.* 3: 1. [48] *Ibid.* 3: 2.

Hosea was profoundly aware of the Mosaic past and looked back with nostalgia to the beginning of Israel's tradition, to the desert, to the 'days of her youth' [49] and to the Covenant.[50] The baneful influence of a materialistic society had caused Israel to forget Yahweh [51]; so Yahweh will bring her back into the desert and speak to her heart.[52] Hosea was the first to represent the covenant relations of Yahweh with his people as a marriage. It is out of his own personal experience that the marriage image came to the prophet, and that he realized its aptness in describing the relations between Yahweh and his people. He understood that the psychology of human love can wonderfully illustrate the mystery of God's relations with men, the reality and depth of his love. The divine husband has been betrayed by his wife who has given herself to adultery and prostitution. Yet he seeks only to win her again to him, and if he chastises her it is with that sole end in view. As a last resort he determines to bring her back once more to the conditions of the Exodus, the honeymoon period of their love.[53] In fact, he ultimately goes beyond this and promises to bring her into the harmony of a new garden of Eden [54] where their love will be the crowning and fulfilment of the mutual love of the first couple.[55]

Hosea has to speak of judgment too and warns of the approaching Assyrian danger.[56] But his leading idea remains the divine goodness (*hesed*) which explains the origin of Israel [57] and which will have the last word.[58] This divine *hesed* is demanding; what God asks is 'steadfast love (*hesed*) and knowledge of God'; [59]

[49] *Hos.* 2: 17 (15).
[50] *Ibid.* 13: 5.
[51] *Ibid.* 13: 6.
[52] *Ibid.* 2: 16 (14); 12: 10.
[53] *Ibid.* 2: 16 f.
[54] *Ibid.* 2: 18.
[55] *Ibid.* 2: 21 f.
[56] *Ibid.* 13: 15.
[57] *Ibid.* 11: 1–9.
[58] *Ibid.* 2: 21 (19).
[59] *Ibid.* 6: 6.

true religion is a practical, loving acceptance of God, an affair of the heart. 'The word *hesed* evokes a relation similar to that denoted by *pietas*; it implies a dedication to someone.' [60]

The God of Isaiah is the 'Holy One'; this holiness, thrice proclaimed by the seraphim, expresses the moral perfection of the deity, but above all, it indicates his inaccessibility and his majesty. Furthermore, for Isaiah, Yahweh is the 'Holy One of Israel'; this transcendent God is a God who acts in history on behalf of his chosen people. The title, by itself, expresses the mystery of an all-holy God who yet stoops down to frail and sinful man.

Isaiah insists on faith—the practical conviction that Yahweh alone matters; one must lean on God alone.[61] He vainly sought, in Ahaz, the faith which would turn the king from human alliances and enable him to stand, unperturbed, in the midst of threats and even in the presence of hostile armies. In place of humble acceptance of God he found wilful self-sufficiency, and he warned Ahaz: 'If you will not believe, surely you will not be established.' [62] This truth is stressed again by Micah who, in his most famous saying [63] presents his message as a synthesis of the preaching of his predecessor and contemporaries: 'He has showed you, O man, what is good; and what does Yahweh require of you but to do justice (Amos), and to love kindness (*hesed*—Hosea) and to walk humbly (Isaiah) with your God?' [64]

It is possible to trace the spiritual progress of Jeremiah and to see in him the purifying and strengthening effect of suffering, for the real message of the prophet is his own life. He was a man of rare sensitivity with an exceptional capacity for affection; and his mission was 'to pluck up and to break down, to destroy and to overthrow' [65] and to cry out, without respite 'violence and destruction' against the people he loved.[66] Jeremiah's efforts

[60] A. Gelin, *Introduction à la Bible I*, 498.
[61] *Is.* 8: 13; 28: 16; 30: 15.
[62] *Ibid.* 7: 9.
[63] *Mic.* 8: 6.
[64] A. Gelin, *op. cit.*, 500. [65] *Jer.* 1: 10. [66] *Ibid.* 20: 8.

to bring his people to their senses failed; but it is the greatness of the man, and the grandeur of his faith, that precisely during the most tragic moment of his life he spoke his optimistic oracles, notably those of chapters 30–33. He saw that the old covenant will be replaced by a new one [67] when God will act directly on the heart of man, when he will write his law on that heart, and when all men will know Yahweh.

> That is one of the epoch-making utterances in the history of religion. Jeremiah had in his youth been a witness of the reformation under Josiah, and had no doubt shared the enthusiasm with which it had been greeted by idealists of the time. It seemed that at last the aim for which good men had striven for a century and a half had been attained. The nation had returned to the Lord their God and sealed their repentance by the solemn acceptance of a high code of social morals such as the prophets had taught. But in the period of disillusionment that followed he came to the conclusion (trite enough by now) that 'you cannot make men good by Act of Parliament.' It was not enough to write good laws into the statute-book. They must be written 'on the hearts' of men. In other words, the only adequate basis for right relations of men with God is in an inward and personal understanding of his demands, an inward and personal response to them. It would not be true to say that Jeremiah first discovered the role of the individual in religion; for it is implicit in all prophetic teaching. But his clear emphasis upon it at the moment when the whole apparatus of public 'institutional' religion had been swept away, was of the first importance for all subsequent development.[68]

Ezekiel showed himself more uncompromisingly still the champion of individual responsibility,[69] and during the first part of his ministry his message was very like that of Jeremiah. After the fall of Jerusalem Ezekiel sought to encourage the exiles and

[67] *Ibid.* 31: 31–34.
[68] C. H. Dodd, *op. cit.*, 46 f.
[69] Cf. *Ezek.* 18: 20.

went about it in his own way. His portrait of the faithful shepherd, the new David, who tends his sheep with justice and love,[70] is not only the inspiration of the passage in *John* 10, but expresses the ideal that will find its realization in Christ. In the promise of a new heart and a new spirit [71] he again approaches Jeremiah.[72] Then, in the last nine chapters of his book [73] he not only describes the New Temple and its rites but goes on to describe the division of the country among the sanctuary, the prince and the twelve tribes. These chapters, from our viewpoint neither very interesting nor very intelligible, have really had more influence than the rest. They express a political and religious ideal that, in large measure, set the pattern for the restoration of Israel.

We shall be content to note two major contributions of Second Isaiah. By his clear-cut and sweeping definition of the concept of ethical monotheism he marked the culmination of the Mosaic movement.[74] And his doctrine of vicarious suffering, as presented in the figure of the servant of Yahweh, not only immeasurably deepened the concept of Messiah but also foreshadowed the Christian victory over suffering: 'In my flesh I complete what is lacking in Christ's afflictions for the sake of his body, that is, the Church.' [75] We have reached the high-point of the prophetic movement, for though the voice of prophecy will be heard until the fourth century, it no longer has the vigour and resonance of the past.

3 THE LAW AND THE PROPHETS

While we must, in the interests of space, leave aside any treatment we may note, at least, the pervasive influence of the law. Throughout the Old Testament the law is everywhere present and it directly or indirectly influences the thought of

[70] *Ibid.* 34.
[71] *Ibid.* 36:23–28.
[72] *Jer.* 31:31–34.
[73] *Ezek.* 40–48.
[74] W. F. Albright, *From the Stone Age to Christianity*, New York, 1957, 327.
[75] *Col.* 1:24.

the sacred writers.[76] The priests are, *ex officio*, guardians of the Torah and specialists in its interpretation [77] and it is their duty to teach the people.[78] Under their authority the Torah developed and was compiled. The prophets recognized the authority of the Torah.[79] Their high moral doctrine was nothing more than a profound understanding of the demands of the Mosaic law. The historians of Israel clearly saw the birth of the nation in the covenant of Sinai. Among them the deuteronomists judged events in the light of the deuteronomical code while the Chronicler was guided in his work by a complete Pentateuch. The wisdom of the sages is enlightened by the Torah, and Sirach states explicitly that the true wisdom is nothing other than the Law.[80] The psalmists extol the law.[81] Finally, Ezra set the Torah as the authoritative rule for the faith and practice of the post-exilic community and as the centre of its life. Attachment to the law inspired the Maccabaean revolt and supported the martyrs and heroes of that rising.

However, we must face the fact that prophetic religion has often been represented as the complete antithesis of priestly religion. It has even been held that the prophets rejected the whole institution of sacrifice and all the ritual of the Temple.[82] Several prophetical texts have been urged in support of these views.[83] An important consideration is that all the prophetical books were finally edited in post-exilic times, when the priestly influence was dominant, and the later compilers and editors are not conscious of any fundamental variance in outlook between priestly and prophetical writings. The Book of Deuteronomy is of paramount interest here. We have noted that it is strongly

[76] P. Grelot, *Vocabulaire de Théologie Biblique*, 544–546.
[77] *Hos.* 5: 1; *Jer.* 18: 18; *Ezek.* 7: 26.
[78] *Deut.* 33: 10; *Hos.* 4: 6; *Jer.* 5: 4 f.
[79] *Hos.* 9: 12; 4: 1 f.; *Jer.* 11: 1–12; *Ezek.* 22: 1–16, 26.
[80] *Sir.* 24: 23, 8; cf. *Bar.* 4: 1.
[81] Cf. *Ps.* 19 (18): 7–14; 119 (118).
[82] The falsity of these views is clearly demonstrated by H. H. Rowley, *The Unity of the Bible*, London, 1953, 30–61.
[83] Cf. *Amos* 5: 21 f., p. 25; *Hos.* 6: 6; *Is.* 1: 11 ff.; *Jer.* 6: 20; 7: 22; *Mic.* 6: 6 ff.

marked by the influence of the prophets, especially Hosea and Jeremiah; yet that book is built around a legal code and regards the existence of a central shrine, with the attendant cult, as a prime article of faith.

When we look again at the passages that allegedly point to a conflict between prophet and priest we find that all of them reflect the unambiguous declaration of Samuel to Saul:

> Has the Lord as great delight in burnt offerings and sacrifices as in obeying the voice of the Lord? Behold, to obey is better than sacrifice, and to harken than the fat of rams.[84]

Here is no rejection of sacrifice but a manifest appreciation of the fact that sacrifice as an external act, unrelated to an attitude of heart, had no value and was an insult to God. It is a measure of the moral perception of Israel that this truth had been clearly grasped at such an early date. Of course, the prophets had to combat formalism in worship, as they had to preach against moral lapses of all kinds, but their stand is a witness to the uncompromising demands of the Law, demands that did not stop at external conformity but which reached to fundamental attitudes. And it was in the Torah that Jesus found the two commandments on which all the law and the prophets depend.[85] The 'great and first commandment' is given in *Deut.* 6: 4 f.: 'You shall love the Lord your God with all your heart, and with all your soul, and with all your might'; and the second is read in *Levit.* 19: 18: 'You shall love your neighbour as yourself.'

All the same, we must admit that the law is much concerned with involuntary acts and ritual uncleanness where no moral considerations were involved, and we must acknowledge that priestly religion did tend towards formalism. In fact, the post-exilic devotion to the law had its dangers, and the tragedy of Judaism is that it ended by succumbing to these dangers.

When we speak of post-exilic Judaism we may not ignore the

[84] 1 *Sam.* 15: 22.
[85] *Matt.* 22: 36–40.

key figure of Ezra for he, more surely than Ezekiel, is the father of Judaism. The 'book of the law of Moses'[86] which Ezra brought from Babylon is most likely the Pentateuch in its final form. This 'book of the law' was accepted by the people as the law of the community, and Ezra, by his cultic and moral reforms, brought the life of the community into conformity with that norm. From this time the life and religion of Jews was directed and moulded by the Torah and Judaism assumed its distinctive characteristic of strict adherence and fidelity to the law.

This does not mean that Ezra is responsible for the extreme legalistic outlook of pharisaism; though it is not altogether surprising that his reform should have led to legalism and isolationism—it is not easy to maintain a balance in such matters. If we are to judge Ezra's role aright we shall need to make certain observations.[87] He did not introduce the emphasis on obedience to the law; that went right back to Moses and the Sinai tradition. Then there is Israel's attitude to the law to be taken into account; the Torah was not regarded as a code to be obeyed, a long list of commands and prohibitions. Rather, it was seen as the will of a law-giver who is the redeemer of Israel; the goodness of God moved the Israelite to serve him freely and to obey him gladly. It follows that the law was not counted as a burden: it was a gracious gift of God and a source of delight.[88] Nor does attachment to the law conflict with the prophetic outlook and spirit. The long prayer of Ezra[89] shows that the post-exilic priestly view was quite in sympathy with the prophetic demands.

In the light of these observations we may appreciate Ezra's attitude to the law and the cult and realize the true place of the Torah in Judaism. If the elaborate Temple ritual did, for many, become an empty form and if devotion to the law lapsed into legalism, these deviations were due to the weakness of Judaism, to the weakness inherent in any community of men. The first

[86] *Neh.* 8: 1.
[87] B. W. Anderson, *op. cit.*, 457–60.
[88] Cf. *Ps.* 1; 19 (18): 7–14; 119 (118).
[89] *Neh.* 9.

manifestation of this weakness was the setting of all precepts, religious and moral, civil and cultic, on the same plane instead of ordering them, in correct hierarchy, around the one precept that would give meaning and life to all of them.[90] As a result the law became the preserve of casuists and became so overloaded with minutiae that it had turned into an insupportable burden.[91] The second danger, and a more insidious one, was to base man's justification on a meticulous observance of the law rather than to visualize it as the work of divine grace, freely bestowed; it meant that man could justify himself. It needed the forceful teaching of St Paul to make clear once for all, that man is not justified by the works of the law, but by faith in Jesus Christ.[92]

4 THE GOSPEL

Paul fully understood and appreciated the truth that the coming of Christ had brought in an entirely new phase of God's dealing with men, a new epoch in *Heilsgeschichte*. The new divine economy is not a continuation of the old along the same plane. Though Christianity strikes its roots deep in Judaism it moves on another level of reality; Christ has made all things new. The regime of the law was transitory, a time of preparation and education, and the law itself was powerless to justify men. Paul not only points to the uselessness (in the Christian era) of the cultic observances of Judaism; he also argues that the moral precepts, within the framework of Judaism, have no real value, while the 'law of Christ' [93] unlike the old law, fulfils the promise of a covenant written on the hearts of men.[94]

Jesus formulated the special character, the new spirit of the Kingdom of God, in the Sermon on the Mount.[95] The new law of Christ does not stand in sharp antithesis [96] to that given on

[90] *Deut.* 6: 4. [91] *Matt.* 23: 4; *Ac.* 15: 10.

[92] *Gal.* 2: 16; *Rom.* 3: 28.

[93] *Gal.* 6: 2; cf. 1 *Cor.* 9: 21.

[94] 2 *Cor.* 3: 3.

[95] *Matt.* 5–7; cf. *Luke* 6: 20–49.

[96] The designation 'antitheses' applied to *Matt.* 5: 21–48 should not be overstressed

Sinai; it is a fulfilment of the Law of Moses.[97] Indeed, Matthew did see the Jesus of the Sermon as a new Moses, but also as more than a Mosaic figure. The Sermon is not another version of the law, it is a definitive formulation. Suggestive of the law of a new Moses, it is also the authoritative word of the Lord, the Messiah; it is the Messianic Torah.[98] We have to be aware, too, that the Sermon is not primarily *kerygma*, a first missionary preaching of the Good News to Jews or pagans [99] but *didache*, a preaching to the Christian community, to those already within the fold. We find in the Sermon on the Mount a compilation of sayings of Jesus which forms an instruction addressed to Christians, one aimed at their Christian formation.

When the Sermon is compared with the rest of the New Testament, it becomes clear that these words of Jesus, his moral teaching, were preserved primarily because they were part of the essential structure of the gospel. Jesus did make demands, he did lay down the law of the Messiah. There is no conflict between gospel and law, the law of Christ. The gospel is not only *kerygma*, not only *kerygma* and *didache*; it is also a moral code, and this was so from the beginning. We might put it another way and say that the *kerygma* includes the acceptance of Christ and of his demands and that the *didache* includes precepts and rules of conduct for Christian living. 'For some in the primitive Church, if not for all, the penetrating demands of Jesus, no less than the great kerygmatic affirmations about him, were part of " the bright light of the Gospel," that is, they were revelatory.' [100] Jesus revealed himself not only in his works and words but also by the exigency of his demands.

We may justly regard the Sermon as a classic example of *didache*. It is a collection of sayings of Jesus, compiled for the purpose of Christian formation, and it most likely served for the instruction of catechumens or for the further direction of the

[97] *Matt.* 5: 17.
[98] W. D. Davies, *The Setting of the Sermon on the Mount*, C.U.P., 1964, 93.
[99] Cf. 1 *Cor.* 15: 3–5.
[100] W. D. Davies, *op. cit.*, 437.

newly baptized. It follows that something is presupposed: the proclamation of the Lord, crucified, risen and to come; the declaration that Jesus has reconciled us with God and that he is our life. What is presupposed is the conquering attraction of the Good News, a sincere conversion; what has already taken place is the witness which Jesus has given, in words and works, to what he is; what is presupposed is faith in the risen Lord.[101]

That is why Jesus is so demanding, that is why he goes so far beyond the law.[102] His teaching is addressed to men who have been rescued by the Good News from the power of Satan, men who already stand in the kingdom of God. He addresses men who have been pardoned, prodigal sons who have been received back into the house of their Father. Men who have received that gift and who have experienced the love and mercy of God, are urged, by inner compulsion, to do the will of that heavenly Father. The commandments of Christ are not further reminders of our sin,[103] but carry with them the divine help that enables us to obey, and the possibility of living as children of God.

The Sermon on the Mount shows us the spirit and the demands of the gospel of Jesus, demands far more exacting than those of the law and a spirit of freedom unknown to the most sincere observer of the law. Above all, he who listens to the demands of Christ, and earnestly seeks to carry them out, is given the means to achieve that task, the liberal gift of grace. Here we put our finger on the difference between law and gospel. The law makes demands, but does not, itself, give the means of carrying them out; it leaves man to himself; the gospel sets man before the gift of God (salvation through Jesus Christ) and demands of him that he should make that ineffable gift the sole foundation of his life. Yet, in the new life there is still room for precepts, there is still need for law, the ' law of Christ.' [104]

Since, however, the quality that Jesus looks for in a faithful

[101] J. Jeremias, *Paroles de Jésus*, Cerf. Paris, 1963, 15–48.
[102] Cf. *Matt.* 5: 21–48.
[103] Cf. *Rom.* 7: 7–13.
[104] *Gal.* 6: 2.

disciple is a boundless love, we may (in the language of John) claim that Christ has given not a law but a commandment.[105] In the Good Samaritan he has taught the lesson in a way that may not be mistaken and cannot be forgotten.[106] He implies that the lawyer's question, 'Who is my neighbour?' has no place in the Christian life. True charity does not pause to weigh up matters of colour or race or creed, but goes without reserve to one in need. The Christian's neighbour is Everyman; his love can have no limits.

But Christian love has deeper reaches still. The true disciple, like the woman who was a sinner, is conscious of being the recipient of great mercy[107] and the effect of this realization is underlined, by contrast, in the Unmerciful Servant.[108] A man who has been freed of a crippling burden, who has experienced the wonder of divine forgiveness, must surely feel compelled to pardon the trifling offences of others. 'Love is not resentful . . . love bears all things';[109] otherwise it is not love. The charity of Christ is the inspiration, and the stuff, of Christian life and of Christian living.

[105] *John* 13: 34; 15: 12; 1 *John* 2: 7 f.
[106] *Luke* 10: 30–37.
[107] *Ibid.* 7: 47.
[108] *Matt.* 18: 23–35.
[109] 1 *Cor.* 15: 5, 7.

THE BLESSED TRINITY
AND THE CHRISTIAN LIFE

John J. Greehy

Since we now have available in English a work of Père Spicq, the distinguished Fribourg professor, on this subject in St Paul [1] I have in fact decided to consider it with St John particularly in mind. Such preferential treatment is given to John because his has been called the 'spiritual gospel'; and coming at the end of the apostolic period, it is also the most profound.

In the twentieth chapter of St John's Gospel we find a theological climax: the confession of Thomas, a recognition of Jesus as his heavenly Lord and God. Of course, the evangelist himself had stated this fact already at the very beginning of his Prologue. It is always refreshing to find the conclusion enuntiated at the very beginning. We really know where we are going. 'My Lord and my God! Jesus said to him, Have you believed because you have seen me? Blessed are those who have not seen and yet believe.' This is not really a comparison but a teaching for the faithful of all times. We are blessed because our faith in the risen Christ, through the word of the eye-witnesses, still living in the preaching of the Church, has the same result as theirs. It leads to eternal life (*John* 15: 26 f.; 17: 20). We might recall the First Epistle of Peter. 'Without having seen him you

[1] *The Trinity and our Moral Life according to St Paul*, by Ceslaus Spicq, O.P., The Newman Press, Westminster, Md., 1963. The same translation, by Sister Marie Aquinas, O.P., has been published in paperback form by Gill and Son, Dublin, 1964, under the title *Saint Paul and Christian Living*. Page references are to this second publication.

love him; though you do not now see him, you believe in him, and rejoice with unutterable and exalted joy. As the outcome of your faith, you obtain the salvation of your souls' (1 *Pet.* 1: 8–9).

John makes it clear that this message gives us the whole point of his writing in what we call the 'first conclusion' to his Gospel (*John* 20: 30–31). 'Now Jesus did many other signs in the presence of the disciples which are not written in this book . . .' A conventional statement of the time, without doubt; but let us not too easily speak of Semitic exaggeration. I quote Professor Dodd in his work on the Johannine tradition. 'Our evangelist, in fact, is to be taken seriously when he says that he selected out of a large number of stories about Jesus those which had relevance to his particular aim.'[2] 'But these are written that you may believe (or be confirmed in your belief) that Jesus is the Christ, the Son of God, and that believing you may have life in his name.' A living faith in the person of Jesus, as redeemer and son of God, leads to eternal life. This is the divine plan of the Incarnation stated in the parables of the Good Shepherd, 'I came that they may have life, and have it abundantly' (*John* 10: 10); and again at the beginning of the Prayer of Intercession, 'Thou hast given him power over all flesh, to give eternal life to all whom thou hast given him' (*John* 17: 2).

THE INITIATIVE OF THE FATHER

It is the Father who begins this giving. He is, first of all, the saviour. We are simply beneficiaries. We are saved through no merit of ours. St Paul tells us in his wonderful account of the mystery of God's will, 'God who is rich in mercy out of the great love with which he loved us, even when we were dead through our trespasses, made us alive together with Christ, and raised us up with him . . . by grace you have been saved through faith, and this is not your own doing; it is the gift

[2] C. H. Dodd, *Historical Tradition in the Fourth Gospel*, C.U.P., 1963, 216, footnote.

of God' (*Eph.* 2: 4–8). The Nicodemus discourse enters its final stage, be it historical word of Jesus or later inspired reflection, with the words, 'For God so loved the world that he gave his only son, that whoever believes in him should not perish, but have eternal life' (*John* 3: 16).

We ask, 'What is this eternal life, given us by the Father?' The Prayer of Intercession continues, 'And this is eternal life, that they may know thee, the only true God, and Jesus Christ whom thou hast sent' (*John* 17: 3). This knowledge is not just an acceptance of a historical Jesus. Admittedly such an intellectual element is present. The seven signs of the First Part call for an intellectual acceptance, but the author of the Fourth Gospel and First Epistle of John, as in the Old Testament, uses the term 'knowledge' as an acceptance by the whole man of the known God. The will, as well as the intellect, responds to God's revelation of himself. Though one can never exclude the intellectual element therefore, the voluntary element remains essential, the observance of commands, charity. 'By this we may be sure that we know him, if we keep his commandments' (1 *John* 2: 3–6). If we have received the gift of life from the Father, we should abide in that life. How are we to do this? 'He who says he abides in him, ought to walk in the same way in which he walked.' We show our response to God's loving-kindness by our imitation of Jesus Christ. The constant *Deo Gratias* of the Pauline epistles is also given concrete form by a call to a life in Christ Jesus. Such a virtuous life gives thanks to God because we use grace for the end which God has assigned it, his own glory. I quote Père Spicq: 'Fidelity to the divine will is nothing other than a long expression of gratitude.' [3] This, it may be added, is the beginning of the life of heaven.

JESUS AS THE LIFE

We must consider the person of Jesus in the Christian's life. In what is almost certainly the primitive kerygma, the first

[3] *Op. cit.*, 36.

proclamation of the Good News, in the early chapters of *Acts of the Apostles*, the person of the crucified and risen Jesus is presented by the authoritative eye-witnesses as the object of *metanoia*, a total change of thinking and conduct to the way of God. This is made concrete in the aggregation to the Christian community by the reception of baptism. The Prologue of the Fourth Gospel tells the story of the rejection by many of God's definitive revelation of himself in the person of Jesus. The Word, identical with the Father, yet distinct, creator of the world, was also the life of men. This key-concept of the whole gospel I take to mean, as in its other fifty usages, supernatural, divine, eternal life. This life is shown in its effect, light. The word 'light' from its Old Testament usage [*Ps.* 26 (27); *Is.* 49: 6] means salvation and happiness, certainly; but also, in view of context and background, it seems that John uses the term primarily to describe the Word, because truth comes through him, and so an 'ethical' element is also involved. This possibility of supernatural enlightenment shines for all time in the world which lacks it (the darkness). Yet men who walked in darkness (*Is.* 9: 2) would not grasp the light, which is truth, salvation, happiness, the effect of the divine life communicated to men by the Word. However, there would always be some who would receive the true light which, entering into the world, enlightens every man. They would be those who would accept the person, mission, commands of the Word of God. They would be transferred, transformed into a new mode of existence. They would be made children of God owing, not to any type of natural, physical generation, but owing to the supernatural power of God, and this through the birth of water and the Spirit (*John* 3: 5). Jesus is the fullness of grace and truth. Of grace, for in him, the only begotten Son of the Father, there is perfectly revealed the divine benevolence towards men, and because he himself is full of the divine life, through him the fullness of salvation is offered to them by means of living faith. Of truth, for he is the incarnate fidelity of God to his promises. He is the definitive norm for our living. An acceptance of this truth will free us from the slavery of sin, and give us the supernatural life of grace. The glory which the disciples saw was God revealed as love in his incarnate Word.

The Gospel of St John tells the story of the acceptance or rejection of God's Word on the part of all types of people. At times the evangelist uses the literary form of a judicial process. The theme is always the same. We would describe it as, 'Nature shows itself in action.' Those who reject Christ (the Jewish leaders) are of the world, used here in a pejorative sense. They live in the way of the world opposed to God. Jesus, and those who follow him, are from God. They do the things of God. There will always be tension between the Word of God, and the world. Now, even though we can use the expression 'realized eschatology' to describe the Johannine writings, that is, the first acceptance or rejection of the Word leads to salvation or condemnation here and now; there is always present the element of 'parousiac' eschatology. (The adjective is current, though it does seem a misuse of the English language!) It means at least this: the fulfilment is not quite yet. There is still much to be done in our present life to ensure our final glory. If this were not the case, there would have been no need for the many homilies against the things of this world, which I consider lie behind what we know as the First Epistle. John warns his Christians who have accepted Christ and profess to follow him: 'Do not love the world or the things in the world. If anyone loves the world, love for the Father is not in him. For all that is in the world, the lust of the flesh and the lust of the eyes and the pride of life, is not of the Father but is of the world. And the world passes away, and the lust of it; but he who does the will of God abides forever' (1 *John* 2: 15–17). We will possess eternal glory, only if we persevere in the will of God.

Our way in such perseverance is Jesus Christ. Our closer following of him will lead us to an ever deeper intimacy with the Father. 'I am the light of the world; he who follows me will not walk in darkness, but will have the light of life' (*John* 8: 12). 'I am the way, and the truth, and the life; no one comes to the Father but by me' (*John* 14: 6). The Christian way is the way of Christ; the way which gives us the life of God here. And this is the way of love.

Two texts of St Paul are particularly relevant here. The first, *Rom.* 6, is not fully developed in the work of Père Spicq. The second, *Col.* 3: 1-4, is just quoted at the end of the book.

St Paul, in *Rom.* 6, points out that it is foolish of us, who have been justified, separated from the world of sin, to involve ourselves in sin afterwards. Here it should be noted that when Paul speaks of the justice of God and our justification, he means that God has been faithful to his promises in choosing, calling us to a life of union with him.[4] He speaks of our real involvement in the mysteries of Christ. We have been baptized into a union with Christ, who died for us, a death which still conditions effectively the same exalted Christ. 'We were buried therefore with him by baptism into death, so that as Christ was raised from the dead, we too might walk in newness of life' (*Rom.* 6: 4).

This 'newness of life' has three aspects. (1) The new life given to Christ as he was raised from the tomb. (2) That participation of the new life of Christ, which is conferred on the faithful in baptism. (3) A new life in the moral order, which the faithful are bound to live. 'If we have died with Christ, we believe that we shall also live with him.' This future refers not so much to future glory (also corporeal) in heaven as to the new life of Christ in which we participate on earth. This new life in the risen Christ, given us in baptism, ought to grow even to the last moment of our earthly existence. We must remain dead to sin and alive to God in Christ Jesus all our lives. There follows the moral exhortation, the consequence of the dogmatic fact. 'Let not sin, therefore, reign in your mortal bodies, to make you obey their passions' (*Ibid.* 6: 12). The death to sin and newness of life must be progressive.

The moral part of *Colossians* begins with the third chapter. If,

[4] Cf. S. Lyonnet, S.J., 'De notione "iustitiae Dei" apud S. Paulum,' *Verbum Domini* (1964), 121–52.

then, you Christians rose with Christ at the precise moment of your baptism, then you ought to seek the things which are above, where Christ is in perfect glory. Such things are enumerated in the twelfth verse: compassion, kindness, meekness, patience. 'And above all these put on love, which binds everything together in perfect harmony' (fourteenth verse). Set your mind on heavenly things, not on things of earth. These latter are listed in the fifth verse: immorality, impurity, passion, evil desire, covetousness. A Christian lives in the world of such things, unquestionably; but he should live his heavenly life in it. 'Our commonwealth is in heaven' Paul tells the Philippians, proud of their *Ius Italicum*. If we conduct ourselves according to the law of heavenly citizens, then we can await with joy the coming of our saviour (*Phil.* 3: 20). This is the prayer of the Fourth Sunday after Pentecost: 'Give to your people to love that which you command, to desire that which you promise, so that among the pleasures of the world, our hearts may be fixed where true joy is to be found.' We Christians have died in baptism, and our life remains hidden with Christ until his coming. When Christ appears in glory, then we shall appear likewise. Our participation in the life of the risen Christ here, which we call grace, is hidden glory. A continuous growth in this grace, by an ever-increasing involvement in the things which are heavenly, leads inevitably to the crowning glory which will be ours in heaven.

St Paul shows us that in everything we do our supreme exemplar is Christ, who effects the life of God in us. Whatever we do must be like the thought of Christ. Thus, when Paul appeals for unity among the Philippians he tells them, 'Have this mind in you which was in Christ Jesus, who, though he was in the form of God, did not count equality with God a thing to be grasped' (*Phil.* 2: 5). Life in Christ is a life of thinking, willing, acting in a Christian way. It is the imitation of Christ. 'For to me, to live is Christ' (*Ibid.* 1: 21). Every Christian is called in baptism to be another Christ. We must seek continuously throughout our lives to follow Christ more nearly. It was under the guidance of the Spirit that Luke differed from the other Synoptics in giving the Word of the Cross a universal interpretation. 'If anyone will come after me, let him deny himself, and take up his cross daily, and follow me' (*Luke* 9: 23).

THE WAY OF LOVE

Let us turn again to the writings of St John. Here the following of Christ is the way of love; and this because God is love. We know the love of God for us especially in the Incarnation of his Son. Without our loving response to this love we cannot know God. 'God is love, and he who abides in love abides in God, and God abides in him' (1 *John* 4: 16). The reason for such response lies in his loving us and sending his Son to be the expiation for our sins (1 *John* 4: 10). This love must be practical. 'If God so loves us, we also ought to love one another.' This compensates for our lack of vision of God in this life. 'No man has ever seen God; if we love one another, God abides in us, and his love is perfected in us.' The more our charity increases, the more we progress in our knowledge of God through the likeness of love.

The love of God and love of our brethren cannot be separated. Our Lord is the supreme example. 'Greater love has no man than this, that a man lay down his life for his friends' (*John* 15: 13). The First Epistle of John is strikingly blunt: 'If anyone has the world's goods and sees his brother in need, yet closes his heart against him, how does God's love abide in him? Little children, let us not love in word or speech but in deed and in truth' (1 *John* 3: 17–18). In *Luke* we find the Master teaching the love of God and the neighbour in the parable of the Good Samaritan, completely exemplified in himself, the universal saviour (*Luke* 10).

Charity, of course, sums up all the commandments. This explains the lack of a Sermon on the Mount or a list of Pauline precepts in *John*. (The other virtues are expressions of charity which informs them). 'If you love me,' says Christ, 'you will keep my commandments' (*John* 14: 15). Obedience to God's will as revealed to men is basic in the Christian life. The fuller the obedience, the greater the advance in the love of God. From recent studies it seems very probable that this sentence of Christ is set in the deuteronomic love of service, which was influenced by the ancient sovereign-vassal terminology of love.[5] Observance of the commandments is the test of true *agape*. The commandments are not to be seen as obstacles to liberty, but as a chance to prove our friendship with the good God. Such a life in accordance with God's revelation makes our light shine before men (*Matt.* 5: 16). This was also the purpose of God's choice of the ancient Israelites. Jesus prays that through the word and work of the Church, the world may believe that the Father has sent him (*John* 17: 20–22). All this thought is echoed by Pope Paul VI in *Ecclesiam Suam*. 'We consider that charity should assume today its rightful position, that is, the first and the highest, in the scale of religious and moral values, not only in theoretical estimation, but also by being put into practice in the Christian life. Let this be so of the charity towards God, who poured out his charity upon us, and true also of the charity which in return we should display towards our neighbours, that is to say, the human race.'

THE SPIRIT OF SONSHIP

In a very valuable chapter Père Spicq treats of the work of the Holy Spirit. A summary follows.

Christians live in Christ Jesus and imitate his virtues, especially charity. Thus they serve God, expressing their gratitude to him and giving him glory. Owing to the difficulties of our experience, however, the Holy Spirit comes to help our weakness (*Rom.* 8: 26). He is received at the moment of baptism when the Christian is adopted as son of God. He comes at the intercession of the Son (*John* 14: 16–26). He is the source of the spiritual life, so that the new morality, contrasting with Israelite morality, is

[5] Cf. W. L. Moran, S.J., 'The Ancient Near-Eastern Background of the Love of God in Deuteronomy,' *Catholic Biblical Quarterly* (1963), 77–87.

a life that responds to the movement of the Holy Spirit. He gives us the power, which the external law can never do, of remaining faithful to God. The law of the Spirit is action according to the spirit (*Gal.* 5: 18). We render service to God which is new and according to the Spirit (*Rom.* 7: 6). The economy of the new alliance is specifically different from the old. If we are incorporated with Christ, we are sealed by the Spirit.

We have the Spirit of filiation then, and do not act as slaves. We are educated to a fulfilment of Christian obligations by the Holy Spirit in person. He gives us a Christian mentality. We adopt, under his influence, the attitude of a son. So we have a morality of sonship. 'A morality of the commandments, even one dictated by sublime motives, imposes a fixed line of action from the outside; but Christians, sons of God, can decide for themselves, supported by a certitude and strength that the Holy Spirit continually infuses into them.' [6] Man's faculty of the divine enables him to know the will of God (*Rom.* 12: 2), and to apply it to his daily life. *Gal.* 5 contrasts actions prompted by sensuality and the fruits of the Spirit. The Christian life is a continual tension between the demands of the flesh and the will of God, between slavery to sin and filial love. The work of the Spirit consists in progressively making us more spiritual. We continually pass from one world to the other. The morality of the Holy Spirit is one of sanctity, or consecration to God. It is also, one of liberty. 'You were called to freedom, brethren' (*Gal.* 5: 13). The Christian life is free owing to the Holy Spirit, and the grace of God. The Christian observes a law of grace, or of Christ dwelling within him. He is subject to the law of the Spirit which gives life. Christians act freely. We are led to think as God thinks, and to act as he acts, out of love. This is the law of charity (*Gal.* 5: 14). Charity is perfection itself, and gives value to all the other virtues which it unites (*Col.* 3: 14). If we stress faith in the writings of Paul, we must remember that it works through love (*Gal.* 5: 6). 1 *Cor.* 13 is a hymn to the value of charity.

[6] *Op. cit.*, 63.

This love, the love God has for us in Christ, given us by the Holy Spirit, makes us capable of the same kind of love as God himself. Under his light we see the love of God in the person of Jesus. The love of Christ for us on the cross engenders our love for him. Charity is an impelling force in all that we do. It makes us like to God. This love is shown in the service of our neighbour. Only this can prove our gratitude to God. Charity, which unites the individual to Christ, will also bind the Christian community together. Fraternal charity builds up the entire Church, as well as the individual soul.

The adaptation on the part of Christians to the changeable circumstances of daily life requires good judgment, keen moral instinct. There is no need for Jewish legalism, covering all possible 'cases,' precepts and interdictions. The Christian has the interior inspiration of the Holy Spirit. 'Conscience assures him real freedom in harmonizing his religious beliefs and his daily living.' [7] We act out of love for God rather than fear of punishment. St Paul does, however, presuppose the demands of the law and of commonsense. This, in the new dispensation, is not propriety, but it is spiritual, because it is done in accordance with the Spirit; and it is this which counts. Through the Spirit Christians judge everything in a Christian way. They advance in the moral life according as they are more or less docile to the Spirit. They can receive God's life in increasing abundance. They can become more spiritual. They approach the perfection of the heavenly Father, enlightened, entreated, strengthened by the Holy Spirit. It may be added here that morality in the Synoptics is not always merely eschatological. It has another aspect. Christians are called to be perfect, as their heavenly Father is perfect, who makes his sun to rise on evil and on good (*Matt.* 5: 43–8). Some of the Synoptic precepts are motivated by the sanctity of the Father.

[7] *Op. cit.*, 73.

LIBERTY AND LAW

There are certain statements in the foregoing analysis of Pauline spiritual morality which require some further explanation. Again, I rely mainly on *John*. If we call the law of the Spirit the law of liberty, then what do we mean by liberty? First of all, we must admit a freedom of the sons of God. ' The truth shall make you free,' said the Lord (*John* 8: 32). Our living acceptance of the incarnate revelation of God, who is Jesus Christ, gains for us the divine life of grace. We are no longer slaves to sin. It is obvious that we should not allow ourselves to fall again under its subjection. To quote *Gal.* 5: 13–16: ' For you were called to freedom, brethren, only do not use your freedom as an opportunity for the flesh, but through love be servants of one another. For the whole law is fulfilled in one word, You shall love your neighbour as yourself. But if you bite and devour one another, take care that you are not consumed by one another. But I say, walk by the Spirit, and do not gratify the desires of the flesh.' All this seems very Johannine, but that is because it is very Christian.

Secondly, how do we understand the liberty from the law in St Paul? This certainly does not mean licence. If Paul says in *Rom.* 6: 14, ' sin will have no dominion over you, since you are not under law but under grace,' he immediately asks, ' What then? Are we to sin because we are not under law but under grace? ' and promptly replies, ' By no means! Do you not know that if you yield yourselves to anyone as obedient slaves, you are slaves of the one whom you obey, either of sin, which leads to death, or of obedience, which leads to righteousness? ' It is important to consider the ancient law, far from the heat of Pauline polemic and Jewish ' legalism,' in the Fourth Gospel comparisons. Jesus is the fulfilment and perfection of the law, which had its own earlier hope-filling function. ' I have not come to abolish, but to fulfil ' (*Matt.* 5: 17). When the Prologue states, ' For the law was given through Moses; grace and truth came through Jesus Christ,' we have, in the words of Professor Jeremias, not so much an antithesis as a crescendo.[8]

[8] A phrase used in a Cadbury lecture at Birmingham University, October 1961.

We find ourselves, then, under the new law of Christ, the perfect revelation of God, and helped by the Holy Spirit in our decisions, who guides us interiorly through conscience. Is there any place in this new economy for external law and authority? Paul himself found it necessary to make his own authority very definite when writing to the Corinthians. He had to combat very strenuously the pretensions of the so-called 'Faction of Christ,' who refused to subject themselves to the authority of the apostles, claiming that they were servants of Christ alone. If in his First Epistle St John says, 'But the anointing which you received from him abides in you, and you have no need that anyone should teach you' (1 *John* 2: 27), he had already just stated, 'Let what you heard from the beginning abide in you.' If it does, 'then you will abide in the Son and in the Father' (*Ibid.* 2: 24). The Spirit of truth who dwells in Christians and teaches them all things (*John* 14: 17, 26), guides them in listening to the teaching authority of the chosen witnesses; and thus they remain free from the error of sin and have divine life. No further teaching about basic doctrines is necessary. We distinguish between the spirit of truth and the spirit of error, if we listen to such authority as has been vested in John. 'Whoever knows God listens to us, and he who is not of God does not listen to us' (1 *John* 4: 6). 'He who hears you hears me,' is the Synoptic statement (*Luke* 10, 16). This apostolic authority extends to the solution of particular cases, at times. St Paul solved many problems in 1 *Cor*., even down to the question of headgear for ladies in church! Authority in the Church has been instituted by Christ. It is moreover an expression of his love for us. It eliminates doubt, ensuring that at all times we are directed on the right road towards God. Such exercise of legitimate authority within the Church, needless to say, is a ministry of love.

For some, external law is very necessary: those who easily reject positive grace in favour of things opposed to God's will. Such law states the limits of friendship or enmity with God. For others, who are growing in the spiritual life, the pressures of the world, the flesh, and the devil may always obscure the instinct of the Spirit. For them external law is not only useful, but also necessary. We are all too conscious of weakness in our Christian living. The external law makes the basic duties of the Christian clear. Then the spirit of Christ moves us not only towards the fulfilment of the precepts of the law, laid down in the external forum and for all of us, but also beyond the limits of law, he leads each of us individually towards what is perfect. Such an activity is not merely for the benefit of each one alone, but for that of all the mystical body.[9]

We must not forget that the Christian life is a gradual development to full liberty. There is a growth from fear of punishment to action through love. God gives salvation freely. He imposes fidelity to his commands, and all commands in our human situations are useless without sanction. Such sanction is a necessary stimulus to some men, that they may 'know' him. Our response to the helping Spirit, however, can lead us gradually to action motivated by love. And 'perfect love casts out fear. For fear has to do with punishment, but he who fears is not perfected in love' (1 *John* 4: 17–18). All action in accordance with God's will, so that we become more and more like to God in Christ, is permeated with our Christian hope in a heavenly fulfilment. If St Matthew says, 'Blessed are the pure of heart for they shall see God' (*Matt.* 5: 8), St John affirms, 'We know that when he appears we shall be like him, for we shall see him as he is' (1 *John* 3: 2).

The Fourth Gospel is the spiritual gospel. It is also a sacrificial, sacramental gospel, and one which asserts the existence of ecclesiastical authority. Through sacrifice, sacrament, and Church teaching, the Spirit guides us to the freedom of the sons of God from sin and ancient, transitory observance.

It is not for me to outline the boundaries of moral and ascetic theology. When the New Testament was written, no such division into separate sciences was contemplated. If in *Gal.* 5 Paul condemns on the one hand the works of the flesh: impurity,

[9] Cf. J. Fuchs, S.J., *Theologia Moralis Generalis, Pars Prima*, Gregorian University Press, 1963, 95.

strife, drunkenness; on the other he extols the fruits of the Spirit: love, joy, peace. Our continual struggle against temptation to sin means a growth in the very same life. A doctrine of the Christian life must always seek to encourage this development unto the fulfilment of glory.

This stress on the invitation of the Father to a way of life in the imitation of his Christ, guided by the Holy Spirit, must be of value in our preaching and catechetics. It is, at least, as necessary and salutary to state the Good News in this way, as to speak of a list of obligations imposed on fearful subjects by a God exacting 'justice.' If we fear to preach the God and law of love, we tend to undervalue the work of the Spirit in Christian souls, who, from the moment of their baptism, draws them to the following of Jesus Christ, who is 'the way, and the truth, and the life.'

THE LAW OF CHRIST

Joseph Fuchs, S.J.

Christian moral teaching, if it is to remain true to itself, must be careful not to give the impression that the Christian message and Christian existence are primarily a matter of ethics. The work of Christ is not meant to proclaim a higher moral standard, but rather salvation, which the love of the Father grants us through Christ. The work of him, who first loved us, sending us his Son that we might live through him (*John* 3: 1–3), should so permeate Christians that their lives and their life's work flow out from the fullness of salvation which was bestowed on them. In this way Christian morality will prove to be the Spirit of the Lord, a spirit which works primarily from within, where it lives as the gift of the Lord, and secondarily finds expression in the prescriptions and commandments which concern men and women who are called in Christ; both together, the Spirit of Christ, living and working in us, and the same Spirit, expressed in prescriptions and commandments, constitute the law of Christ.

What St Paul says of the new law of Christ as compared to the law of the Old Testament is said as *per typum*. Every law given by God is holy and divinely great (*Rom.* 7: 12; *Tim.* 1: 8), but nevertheless is only leading to Christ (*Gal.* 3: 24) and finds its fulfilment in him (*Rom.* 10: 4). Now only Christ matters, the crucified and risen Christ; he is our salvation and our law (*Gal.* 6: 2; *Cor.* 9: 21). No other law can be of any value, unless it be subsumed in Christ and thus become the law of Christ. And it can only have been of value in history insofar as it virtually and fundamentally contained the law of Christ, as Thomas Aquinas says of the law of the Old Testament and of the natural law in its relation to the history of salvation.

When therefore at certain periods (not only in our days, but also, for instance, in the German theology of morals in the last century) Christian ethics become particularly conscious of their Christian character, they search for the Spirit of Christ, which should form our lives, this Spirit as we know it from the Scriptures, from tradition and from theology. Again and again the same twofold question is put to the current moral doctrine: (*a*) whether it is not based too exclusively on a philosophical anthropology, which sees man only as a being made to serve his Creator, and hardly at all as one who is lost in sin and receives justification and law from the Spirit of our Lord; (*b*) whether it does not stress too much a philosophical order, that is, an order of natural law, and neglects the Spirit of Christ, which after all determines the life of man, who has been born 'in the flesh' (sarx) in sin, but has been justified and saved 'in the spirit' (pneuma) in Christ. Within recent decades we have experienced such a re-appraisal with, on the one hand, its positive side, namely an enrichment through the appreciation of some Christian values often insufficiently perceived or, at any rate, reflected upon; and, on the other hand, its negative side, the danger of an unjustified exclusion of the absolute duty of the created being to its Creator and of the order of creation expressed in natural law.

Joy in Christ and in his law sometimes encourages the Christian to compare this law with the law of non-Christians, as if there existed a twofold moral law, one for Christians and another one for non-Christians, for the latter maybe even a purely natural law. Yet the conception which makes such a comparison, is guilty of an under-valuation of the law of Christ. Rather might one compare it with a purely natural moral law, if such a thing existed—which it does not. I agree that there is a natural order of creation, a natural moral law, but it does not stand by itself; it is part of the whole, the order and the law of Christ. Therefore, there is only one single law for all men, the law of Christ. It is the law for man, who is saved from the slavery of sin, justified by grace, and lives in the Church of our Lord. This is the human being and there is no other in the divine decree, except perhaps the one in whom (whether or not through his own fault) God's plan for man is only imperfectly realized, such as, for instance, the man who is ignorant, the sinner, the unbelieving man. Just as there is only one final destiny for all, which is to be heirs of the Father and co-heirs of Christ (*Rom.* 8: 17; *Gal.* 4: 6), so there is also for all only one way and one law, which is Christ. Objectively, these are the facts, even though subjectively a man can and must pursue this way and live this law according to his subjective ability or, in other words, according to the degree in which he is near to Christ and knows him.

When we speak of the law of Christ, we must first of all pay attention to the fact that he himself, the person of Christ, is our law, the pattern of our life, its basis; secondly, we must consider in which way and precisely in which sense Christ can truly be and is our law; and thirdly we must specially take note of the relation between the law of Christ and the moral natural law.

THE PERSON OF CHRIST AS PATTERN AND LAW

A true understanding of the plan of salvation, in the light of Holy Scripture, enables us to see that the eternal God willed his Christ, the God-man, so that he could be the 'firstborn amongst many brethren' (*Rom.* 8: 24). Therefore he let him be the 'firstborn amongst the dead' (*Col.* 1: 18). He willed that all fullness should dwell in him and that so he should have the primacy (*Col.* 1: 28; *Eph.* 1: 22). Therefore, he is the fullness and original pattern of all who die in sin and are called to a new life.

Further, if in the light of an exegesis which is constantly gaining ground, we are to understand the Christ of the letter to the Colossians as the *Christus* and not only as the *Verbum*, then we see that this Christ, the God-man, was already the original picture, in whom and towards whom everything, particularly man, was created, so that he might be the 'firstborn of all creation,' in whom and through whom all is created, and in whom all has its existence (*Col.* 1: 15; cf. also *Cor.* 8: 6; *Eph.* 1: 3–10). For all human and Christian existence, therefore, there is one, who is the archetype, and who as God-man contains in himself all true potentialities of human and Christian existence, namely Christ. From the beginning he was the one towards whom and according to whom all were created, so that he would be the first among many. At his entry into the world, his incarnation, he took into himself historically all human and Christian existence.

Therefore, he is the measure of life for all. Life means more than existing as man; it means living as Christ. One takes as the source and pattern of one's life the reality of Christ, the Son of God who became man, and who was crucified and glorified. Christ is for everyone the measure of his being and thereby also the measure of his life. He is the source and the measure of the grace that comes to everyone, and the source and measure of the being which this grace finds already in existence. For this reason he is for everyone the well-spring and pattern of supernatural morality (in relation to grace) and of natural morality (in relation to one's existence as mere man). When we circumscribe moral life with universal norms, natural and supernatural, we must not forget that these norms are, in the last analysis, derived from the God-man Christ, on whom all human being and all human order is based. If we seek to assess the individuality of each man and of the particular situation in which he finds himself, norms formulated in general terms do not satisfy us. We seek the proper manner of applying these general norms. In this search it strikes us that the individual and everything which makes him a particular being—and so also the moral law which applies to him—are founded on the one Christ. Von Balthasar says quite rightly that our moral life should be measured, in a more radical sense, by the person of Christ rather than by general laws; that our moral duty is more radically expressed as imitation of Christ rather than as observance of general norms, which, of course, are presupposed in the imitation of Christ; and that one's own being grounded on Christ is a more radical guide than universal norms. Therefore, he calls Christ the most concrete norm, because he is an individual person, and at the same time the most universal norm, because he is the measure of each and every person and of every situation.

Seen ontologically Christ is the archetype of each human being, and each by his moral behaviour must endeavour to reflect the Christ in whom he has his existence (*Col.* 1:17). It is not enough to make it one's duty to realize certain moral values or to fulfil abstract moral patterns, but each individual, grounded on the person of Christ, must demonstrate the meaning and value of his commitment. This is all the more true in that Christ has given us, in a historical and approachable way, an example of human life, namely, his life, both individual and conditioned by situations. This does not mean that one who is not the individual Christ can repeat this life—an impossibility—but one can imitate his example in a particular way. We can love God in a way as he loves God (*John* 15: 10), and love our neighbour as he loved us (*John* 13: 34); we can even humbly serve our brother after the example of the one who washed the disciples' feet (*John* 13: 12–15); we can imitate his example of suffering (*Peter* 2: 21) and his manner of walking on this earth (1 *John* 2: 6). We can, with the apostles (1 *Thess.* 1: 6; 1 *Cor.* 11: 1), make Christ's ideas our own (*Phil.* 2: 7; *Rom.* 15: 1–3; *Rom.* 15: 7); and we can have in our life ever before our eyes the glorified Lord who died and who was awakened from the dead (*Rom.* 6) after a life of suffering (2 *Cor.* 1: 5; *Phil.* 3: 10) anguish (*Col.* 1: 24) persecution (2 *Tim.* 3: 12) patience (2 *Thess.* 3: 5) truth (2 *Cor.* 11: 10) and love (*Phil.* 1: 8). Following his example, looking at him, we should imitate him in our way and thereby ' put him on,' (*Rom.* 13: 14). Being able to see and experience the individual example of the absolute, once-for-ever man Jesus Christ, allows us to understand more deeply and truly what is and should be our own personal life—the particular life which for each of us has been created in him and awakened in us out of our death. We can understand more deeply and truly what type of behaviour and what type of attitude is needed, so that any particular situation may be patterned on the original picture of the person of Christ.

Moreover the Christ, who is our archetype and example, has extended to us personal communion with himself so that we can follow him and can share in his destiny (death and resurrection: *Rom.* 6; *John* 12: 26; 17: 14). In order to make it a true discipleship and union of life, he gives us his life and resurrection as our possession (*Rom.* 6), he allows his life (the true vine) to be our life (*John* 15: 5) and he makes us the members of his one body, whose head he is (*Col.* 1: 18). The Christian who knows this community with the Lord, and who is aware of the call to personal following, the call of him 'who first loved me and gave himself up for me' (*Gal.* 2: 20), will learn from the love in which he follows the Lord. This love will teach him, better than an ethic of values or a code of rules, to understand the example of the Lord and the meaning of his own life, a life which is based on the person of Christ as its personal archetype and standard.

THE LAW OF CHRIST AS GRACE AND CHALLENGE

Christ is the standard for the individual human person, for his life and his individual situation in life, since everyone is formed after the God-man Christ. This applies to the individual's concrete mode of existence as a human being, each in his own way and with a particular relationship to his environment; it applies also to the special way in which one has become a sharer in the grace of Christ. We must view grace as giving the highest and final determination to man's being, and so also to his activity. The grace-given being-in-Christ of each individual is being and task, fact and obligation at once. The grace of Christ, considered as the last and highest form of being and the pattern for each one, cannot be taken in an empty and abstract way. It must be viewed as grace forming the individual man, or rather this particular man who comes to the highest fulfilment for which he exists through this precise grace of Christ. The grace of Christ, therefore, as pattern of each one, embraces in the same way also the pattern given in the concrete being of man, precisely as man, that is, the purpose of each individual given to him by natural law. The law of Christ is for this reason an inward law, namely the task imposed on us by our existence in Christ.

Yet grace, especially in the man who shapes his life in a personal and responsible way, must not be understood primarily as something which is in itself. Rather we must see it as power, as the effective activity of the Holy Ghost in us. In this way it becomes clearer than ever, how Christ is our law. The spirit of Christ in us overcomes the demand of the flesh, the egoistical concupiscence of man under original sin, and forms in its place the spiritual man, the man who makes the innermost surrender by striving to be in his own daily life the 'man in Christ,' which he is by the life of Christ.

The grace of the Holy Spirit puts love in the place of the egoism which is caused by original sin. By a deep inner impulse this love presses towards a full presonal realization of human and Christian existence, through which one is grounded in Christ. Therefore, the driving force of our lives as men and as Christians, the driving force of natural and supernatural being, will be felt not as a law which forces us against our inclination (particularly as man under original sin) and in this sense as an outer law. Rather will this driving force be felt as our innermost willing and loving, which is caused in us by the Spirit of Christ of which we are sharers. It is above all in this special sense that the law of Christ is an inner law. To man under original sin, as such, it is not only the law imposed from outside by legislation that appears to him as something contrary and to that extent an outward law; he also finds contrary and outward the law which corresponds to his own being (and is in this sense an inner law, that is, the law of natural and supernatural existence). As long as man remains in the life of the flesh he will more or less remain in this state.

If one is carried by the grace of the spirit of Christ, the imperative of being man-in-Christ will be one's own willing and loving. The more one allows oneself to be caught up by the grace of Christ, the more will this imperative, which is based both on natural law and the supernatural order, become one's own innermost concern, one's inner law. What constitutes the law of Christian life and conduct, is not so much the being and obligation that are derived from Christ, but rather the striving and loving that flow from the grace of the spirit of Christ.

The grace of the spirit of Christ imparts to us above all a participation in the life of Christ, that is, a participation in the love of Christ, with the result that we love as Christ loves. In this way we can describe the love of Christ, which is activated in us by the grace of the Holy Ghost, as the real and inner law of Christ. Whatever this driving love in us, the love of Christ, is able to carry out, is good; and only that is good which can be an expression of this Christian love, which is given to us by grace. One thing is clear however, Christian love in us can carry out and express itself in what truly corresponds to and is demanded by our concrete human existence in Christ, only in so far as this is grounded in the person of Christ. Included in this is the natural law challenge to the individual human being, together with the supernatural demands arising from the order of grace. There is question not only of the general requirements of existence according to the natural and supernatural moral order, but also the concrete demands which follow for each one from the impulsion and call of grace, that the living spirit of Christ makes active in us. This love, which unites us with God, will have made on it many a call and demand, which will surpass the ordinary demands of reason set by the natural law and the ordinary demands of love. In any case all demands made on a believing and loving Christian—even those grounded in natural law—will be understood, willed and made real not only in their own being, but beyond this—at least implicitly and without reflection—as modes of living in Christ before the Father.

Christ therefore becomes law in us, not only in that he in himself and in his formation in us is our ontological measure and pattern, but in that he gives us from within by the action of the grace of his spirit the capacity to will and to love according to this pattern. Christ is our law not so much in acting and demanding from outside (in ways which counter the desires of the man of the flesh), but rather in shaping and guiding the inner man. He is lawgiver not so much because he himself becomes a standard for us, or makes demands of us, but because he overcomes the 'man of the flesh,' and causes in us by grace the fulfilment love demands. Grace is, therefore, in each man the 'spirit of life in Christ Jesus' (*Rom.* 8: 2), which pours out love in us (*Rom.* 5: 5), which helps our weakness (*Rom.* 8: 26), and which moves us from within (*Rom.* 8: 14). The grace of the spirit of Christ therefore is the law of Christ, because it (1) enlightens the Christian so that he can understand the Christian challenge and the call of Christ to each one, and (2) it gives the love which accepts and lives the call of Christ. The grace of the spirit of Christ is not a law set forth before all men in the same way, but a guiding and thereby a law for each single person from within.

This grace is not just a law that remains within the general pattern of universal norms, but a law that leads step by step towards perfection, the fullness of Christ. The law of Christ does not only command this and that particular thing in the same way to all people. It challenges each person entirely according to his possibilities in this particular situation in life under the call of grace.

The law of Christ is primarily grace. As such it enlightens each one, moves him from within and thereby leads him to the perfection which is due to him singly. This law of Christ, as has been said, is not contrary to any outer law, but includes it. The natural moral order, grounded in the being of man, retains its absolute validity under the dynamic force of grace, and the same can be said of the supernatural moral order grounded in our existence in Christ. The commandments in the order of creation (in natural law), which can be formulated and are formulated, and the commandments of the Gospel, as also the positive valid precepts of human authority, all these keep their value within the law of Christ. Yet they are not its primary elements. In themselves they remain outward laws, that is, both the demands of natural law and of the Christian law of love, in the sense that we cannot love and live them from within —all the more, if we remain still ' men of the flesh ' in spite of grace. Thus they are still a law bringing sin and death. Only the grace of the spirit of Christ makes them our inner law, so that we love and live them and thereby live as Christ lived. Again they are only an outward law in the sense that they cannot give a complete picture of how each one is led by grace to the perfection which Christ has destined for him.

This secondary element of the law of Christ—distinct from the grace of the spirit of Christ—the outward law, stands in the closest relation to its primary element, grace. It indicates values and ways of acting in which the impelling power of grace, the love caused by the Holy Ghost, will express itself. The commands of the moral order, which are formulated or could be formulated, show this or that as the task of true human and Christian living. This is their intrinsic meaning. Over and above this, they have a self-transcending sense, for Christ's guidance by grace and Christian love will be a driving force only within these commands and not outside them. They show the Christian who loves God and is led by the Holy Ghost, a way which he must never leave. As outwardly formulated commands they help us to avoid error. We are limited by our condition as *viatores* and by the tendencies of the ' fleshly ' man, which we will always remain in this life. The commandments will help us not to misunderstand the driving power of grace and love, not to interpret it in the manner of a man of ' flesh ' and try to realize it in this manner. In this way the outward law is a help and a salutary constraint, serving the primary element of the law of Christ, the grace of the spirit of Christ within.

Therefore, the Christian moral code will effectively expound, unfold, motivate, and make understandable the commands of the law of Christ, of the Gospel and of the natural order of creation for all Christians and non-Christians. In this way it becomes a guide to the true man and the man-in-Christ. It will point to the person of Christ so that knowing the archetype, and the historical example, and lovingly imitating the Lord who is united with us by grace, we can grasp more deeply the value of the prescriptions and commands. Christian moral teaching must also make clear that even the person of Christ and the demands based on the person of Christ would become for us men under original sin, sin and death, were it not for the working of the grace of the spirit of Christ within us. We can also see that the Lord, leading us within, will indeed move us to an absolute or unchanging observance of his prescriptions and commands. At the same time he will move each individual person along a way towards Christian perfection, which is for him alone. He will lead each on to his particular perfection, which is grounded in the person of Christ and on the call of Christ. Even if the guidance of grace within us and the love caused by God within us do not move us away from the prescriptions of moral order and from precepts, loyalty to these prescriptions and commands must not endanger loyalty to the grace within us. For this grace points to the appropriate manner, spirit and intensity in which the prescriptions and commandments are to be fulfilled by each individual; it points also to something higher than the general order and general rules and commands.

Loyalty to order and pattern, as the secondary element of the Law of Christ, must not turn us away from the primary element, the inward grace of the spirit of Christ, which alone brings about Christian life and its *fulfilment*. This grace within, which in each individual overcomes gradually the ' fleshly ' man, is a personal guidance by the spirit of Christ and leads the ' spiritual ' man on progressively step by step. The systematic setting forth of the prescriptions and commands must not claim to be absolute, but should be done so as to respect the freedom in which the Lord leads and calls each one. This however will not be outside law and order.

THE LAW OF CHRIST AND NATURAL LAW

The question of the natural order of creation, the law of nature, stood out prominently in the treatment of the law of Christ, and had necessarily to stand out, because we had to prove that the Christian moral order lies in the God-*man*. It is of importance to set forth now, expressly, the position of the natural law in relation to the law of Christ.

It is clear that the moral natural law belongs as an integral part to the whole of the Christian moral law. This is clear from the fact that, for instance, both Christ himself and St Paul, neither of whom intends anything but the propagation of Christian morality, press for an observance of natural morality. St Paul propagates the commands of natural morality as belonging to the Evangelium (Gospel) of the Lord. (1 *Thess.* 4: 2; *Phil.* 4: 9; 1 *Cor.* 7: 10). The Church of Christ includes in its preaching, interpretation and defence of the Christian moral teaching, the natural order of creation also. The Christian existence and Christian ordering of our life is founded in Christ as the God-man, and in the fact that the Word of God, entering into the world, became man and thereby our archetype and model (example). Man thus finds himself in an order of things grounded in human nature as such. For this reason, as already remarked, the grace of the spirit of Christ within us compels us to loyalty to the order of creation.

The natural moral law has a definite place within the Christian moral law. In the God-man his ' being man ' should be seen as a substratum, enabling God's Word to dwell amongst us in a human way. Grace and God's revelation presuppose as their ' substratum ' human nature, so that we can well (possibly) assume that ' being man ' is willed by God as ordered to ' being under grace ' or ' being in Christ.' Therefore *quoad se* it is not the natural law which is primary, but the Christian moral law which necessarily implies the natural law, which is, in fact, presupposed by the supernatural law in itself. *Quoad nos* however, the primary place will always be held by the law of nature, to which we see added other moral elements, derived from the supernatural order, from the Word incarnate, from the individual call of grace (*natura*, *non re*, *posterius*). To these elements we have no approach except under the supposition of the natural order of creation.

Within the Christian moral order, the natural law has an immanent meaning that is specific to itself. The natural law speaks of a true human existence and of human values. But because its position is within the order of Christ, it has not only a meaning proper to itself but also a *transcending* meaning—at least if we look at it abstracting from its being in Christ. Concretely, *quoad se* (that is, in the totality of creation, which is precisely not only natural but in fact grounded in Christ) it must not only serve to make one the true human being as such, but before all else the Christian being which obviously demands and includes in itself true human existence. The man who is in fact in Christ, always intends in his behaviour within the natural law more than this natural law, even if he does so without reflection. In it he refers always to Christ, to God the Father, to salvation. He achieves in his conduct according to the natural law something beyond that law, because he does it with an intention that goes beyond the natural level. Acting according to natural law therefore gains, if done 'in Christ,' real salutary power, which as such, abstractly taken, it cannot have.

Examining salvation from the historical viewpoint, one can with good reason say that Christ has redeemed the natural law. Natural law in this sense is an inner inbuilt law; it consists primarily not of outward norms, but is an order particular to man himself, towards which man is fundamentally inclined as right and reasonable. To the man of original sin, insofar as he thinks and strives in a 'carnal' way, the demands of the natural law are disagreeable. They become for him, as we said before, sin and death. They are for him demands from without. The grace of the Saviour, the spirit of Christ within us, turns the natural law to a law of life in that it changes us to men of the spirit, who fulfil lovingly the natural moral order in a Christian life. Over and above this the spirit of Christ helps us—by revelation, Church and grace—to come to the knowledge of the natural order of creation; because this knowledge is placed in jeopardy, largely because of the consequences of the fall. The continuous activity of the spirit of Christ concerning the natural law, its knowledge and fulfilment, shows us how correct it is to see the natural law in the whole of the work of salvation and in the corresponding law of Christ, because the supernatural activity of grace, revelation and Church does not take place for human existence as such.

If we look at the moral order of man as such, namely the natural law, we must never forget that we talk of something in the abstract, because we isolate it from complete reality, the law of Christ. Then we understand that the natural law does not really refer to *natura pura* (which just as *natura lapsa* and and *natura redempta* expresses a definite condition or state of the human being, namely the merely natural state). It refers rather to the specific nature of man, independently of any particular state in which it happens to be realized. This is important for the question of a continuity or discontinuity between natural law and the law of Christ. Is there then a contradiction between these two? Is the natural law being altered under Christ? The fact that certain demands, for example, the Sermon on the Mount, are perceived by us as difficult and demanding sacrifice—and this they certainly are—is due not so much to any tension between the law of Christ and the natural law, as to tension between the law of Christ and the carnal man. The carnal man immediately rebels, and the selfishness imparted by original sin must be corrected by sacrifices before he can fulfil the due order. Man redeemed from the depths of fallen nature will, however, sacrifice genuine human values, precisely in order to attain the lofty level of Christian existence. These values, however, are those of an order of pure nature (*natura pura*). But in fact man has not been created for the condition of pure nature, but essentially to be open to every call of God. He has been created in accordance with the creator's will, with a view to his fulfilment in Christ. A natural law measured on the standard of *natura pura* must find itself limited and reduced by the Gospel; a natural code of ethics measured on the standard of *natura*, of human existence as such, finds in Christ its true fullness of meaning, for which God had intended it from the beginning. It would, therefore, be more correct not to speak, as often happens, of a comparison between the law of Christ and a purely natural ethical order, but rather of the relation of the law of Christ to the natural order of creation, to natural law.

The law of Christ is more than a code of natural law demands; but even the natural law order, when seen in the totality of the law of Christ, goes beyond, transcends itself. By the law of Christ is meant the ethical order which is grounded in the person of Christ and his image in the individual man. Yet the law of Christ is not only, not even primarily, an order which makes demands and has universal validity; it is rather the inner grace of the spirit of Christ, which powerfully leads the individual to form in himself the image of Christ, and to form it in that full measure to which the Lord calls the individual.

LIFE IN CHRIST:
LIFE IN THE CHURCH

Kevin McNamara

Today the doctrine of the Church is at the centre of Christian thought and in a special way, of Catholic thought. From its beginning the Second Vatican Council has concerned itself particularly with clarifying this doctrine and, with the passage of time, has more and more come to see in this its principal task. Pope Paul VI has repeatedly called attention to the growing self-awareness of the Church and to the great spiritual benefits to which it can lead. It is clear that for some considerable time to come the Church's self-understanding which is being formulated by the Council will have a decisive influence on religious life and thought. It seems opportune then, in a Summer School devoted to new trends in moral theology, to ask what light the doctrine concerning the Church can throw on Christian moral teaching.

A few decades ago this would scarcely have seemed a very promising line of investigation. But today a richer doctrine of the Church affords many attractive approaches to such a study. What I hope to do is to take some of the main insights of this renewed ecclesiology and show their application to the Christian life. My purpose is not so much to adduce new support for the developments in moral theology which are being explained in the other lectures; I do not think any such support is necessary, though it is certainly afforded by what I have to say. What I should chiefly hope to do is to suggest a new point of view, a new context for what the moral theologians are telling us today; to link this teaching to some familiar ecclesiological themes and in that way add a little to our understanding of it.

What then is the Church? Today we have rediscovered, or are engaged in rediscovering, several valuable images or descriptions of the Church to supplement the excessively juridical and apologetic treatment of the text-books hitherto in use. Chief amongst them is the image of the body of Christ, which presents the Church as the association of those who through baptism have received community of life and destiny with Christ, and form an organic unity among themselves somewhat after the fashion of the human body. More recently we have become familiar with another idea, that of the people of God, which complements the theme of the body of Christ by stressing the historical roots and development of the Church and calling attention to such important biblical themes as the covenant, the law, the word of God, etc. Again, the Church is commonly seen nowadays as the temple of the Holy Spirit, the 'holy place' in which the spirit of God dwells and gives himself to men, sanctifying them and enabling them to offer true worship to the Father. Another idea offering important insights is that of the kingdom of God. Through the Church God is establishing his rule in the world, setting up his kingdom in the hearts of men and giving it visible and social expression in history, in preparation for its final and perfect realization in the future life.

All these ideas represent very different approaches to the mystery of the Church, and theologians now face the task of integrating them, together with many other themes, into a unified, organically-structured treatise on the Church. As yet this task has scarcely been begun, but nevertheless a fair measure of agreement can be noted on the mutual relationships of the principal themes I have mentioned. More and more theologians are impressed by the advantages of giving the theme of the people of God the fundamental place. This should not be taken to mean that it best expresses the true nature of the Church, but rather that it provides the most suitable starting-point and outline for a treatise *De Ecclesia*. It is in fact only when we consider the other themes I have mentioned, that the unique and mysterious character of the Church, in particular its intimate dependence on Christ, comes truly into view; only then do we see what kind of people God has established, what is the source of its life and the true law of its being. Only then does the image of the Church suggested by the idea of the people of God appear in all its rich significance.

If we adopt this approach, and try to give a fairly comprehensive description of the Church, we could unite and co-ordinate the few ideas I have mentioned somewhat as follows: *The Church is the people of God established by Christ in his body through the power of the Holy Spirit in order to realize the kingdom of God.* Here we make mention first of the calling by God of a special people, then of the condition in which this people exists, namely as the body of Christ, next of the instrumental rôle of the Holy Spirit in fashioning and sustaining it, and finally of the overall purpose of God, namely to establish his kingdom. The starting-point is the idea of the people of God. This will provide us with a number of initial insights into the nature of the Christian life, each of which we shall go on to develop in the light of the full description of the Church which I have given. The Christian life is the life of the people of God, but it is also the life of the members of Christ's body, of those in whom dwells the spirit of God and in and by whom the rule of God is being established. The ancient biblical theme of the people of God leads us first of all to the Old Testament, where we shall find the beginnings of the characteristic features of the way of life which God looks for in those whom he has chosen. Already in the Old Testament God has his people, already, too, his designs for his kingdom are being put into effect. But it is only in the perspectives afforded by the strictly New Testament themes of the body of Christ and temple of the Holy Spirit that the full picture of Christian morality, and especially its distinctive features, can be seen.

A PEOPLE CALLED BY GOD

Let us turn then to the people of God which came into existence when Yahweh called the Israelites out of Egypt and transformed them from a disorganized array of tribes into a unified and ordered nation. In time this people was to yield to the new people of God, which is the Church, but for all the newness of the latter there is continuity between the Old and the New and the characteristics of God's action remain constant. One such characteristic is that God freely chooses his own, without any merit on their part. It was a natural temptation for Israel to believe that it was because of some special excellence on her part that God had chosen her for his own people. But God explicitly warns them against any such pretensions. 'It was not because you were more in number than any other people that the Lord set his love upon you and chose you, for you were the fewest of all peoples, but it is because the Lord loves you, and is keeping the oath which he swore to your fathers, that the Lord has brought you out with a mighty hand, and redeemed you from the house of bondage, from the hand of Pharaoh king of Egypt.' [1] There is no more ultimate reason for God's love and choice of his own than that love itself; he loves and chooses whom he wills himself. The New Testament leaves us in no doubt that this applies also to the new people of God; this people too owes its choice simply to God's love and mercy. 'So it depends not upon man's will or exertion,' St Paul sums up his argument in writing to the Romans, 'but upon God's mercy.' [2] Before the beginning of the world God has chosen us in Christ,[3] not because we were of great account, for it is especially those who are insignificant and foolish in the eyes of men that God delights in calling.[4]

Here we have revealed to us one of the most fundamental truths in regard to the Christian life. It is the simple, but often

[1] *Deut.* 7: 7 f.
[2] *Rom.* 9: 16.
[3] *Eph.* 1: 4.
[4] 1 *Cor.* 1: 26–31. Cf. *Matt.* 11: 25 f.

forgotten, or at any rate not fully appreciated fact that this life is a pure gift of God. We have done nothing to deserve it, and of ourselves we can neither develop nor maintain it. Our contribution is simply to receive it, to accept the gift which is offered to us. The basic attitude which is demanded of us in face of God's approach to us, therefore, is one of receptivity, openness, expectancy. Only if he finds a certain minimum of this spirit in men can God give his gifts, for otherwise they would not be received as gifts but as something due to man, and this would be to deny their true character. In Old Testament times as well as in those of the New Testament, it is this spirit of humble receptivity that God looks for. Man must not look to himself for his salvation but to God. In this rule are included humility, confidence, gratitude, obedience, belief in God's word, hope in him and, inevitably, love; the qualities, in fact, that distinguish that little group so often described in the Old Testament as 'the poor,' and that later figure so largely in our Lord's Beatitudes. It was precisely for lack of this spirit that Christ castigated the Pharisees, who looked to their own righteousness, based on exact observance of legal prescriptions, to justify them before God. In modern times we have become familiar with the phrase 'the way of spiritual childhood,' the name given by St Thérèse of Lisieux to what she called 'her little way,' but what was in reality the heart of the spirituality of the Gospels, which is precisely where Thérèse discovered it. When our Lord looked for faith as the basic requirement of the Christian life, it was not simply intellectual assent to his message that he was seeking, but the general attitude of soul that I have described. This is very obvious once we recall how prominently the idea of confidence in God's power and goodness figures in faith as it appears in the Gospels. For St Paul too faith is essentially an acknowledgment of God's sovereignty, the refusal to glory in oneself or one's good works. 'To have faith,' says Stauffer, 'is to bow the head before the hidden glory of God.' [5] St Paul sums it all up in his

E. Stauffer, *New Testament Theology* (E. tr.), London, 1963, 171.

letter to the Ephesians: 'For by grace you have been saved through faith; and this is not your own doing, it is the gift of God—not because of works, lest any man should boast.'[6]

The supreme example of this humble filial spirit which does not rely upon itself or seek its own glory, has been afforded by Christ himself. This is not surprising, since the people of God, as we have seen, exists in the form of the body of Christ. Christ is the head, we are the members, united with him in a common life and destiny. It is because Christ always sought the glory of the Father and lived out to its extreme implications his condition of absolute dependence on the Father that we too are called, and are given the power, to accept God's favours, to open our souls to grace. To follow Christ, to share in his life, these are the privileges of Christ's members, and a fundamental aspect of this following and this sharing is the spirit of humble dependence. It is Christ himself who will teach us, and who as our head will impart to us this basic constituent in the common life of the people of God. To the extent that he does so we have the remedy, both in our own lives and in the life of the Church as a whole, against a danger of which we have recently been reminded under a new name, but which is as old as the Bible, the danger of 'triumphalism,' which in its extreme form is the same attitude so strongly condemned by Christ in the Pharisees.

In all this Christ will act in the power of the Holy Spirit. The Holy Spirit is in fact the basic gift that we receive, sent by the Father and the Son into the Church at Pentecost to form God's people and into our souls at baptism. With him he brings the Christian life with its attendant virtues and other gifts. Here we are reminded of our fundamental obligation to the spirit of God, that of dependence, of loving attendance on his inspirations, of gratitude for his favours. The Holy Spirit is the bond of love which unites the Son in complete and utter dependence on the Father, and he is come into our souls to give us a share in that loving dependence. The gifts he brings us at baptism are only

[6] *Eph.* 2: 9. For the New Testament notion of faith see R. Schnackenburg, art. 'Glaube,' LThK, IV 915–17.

the beginning. Throughout our life he desires to add to them, that he may lead us to more perfect conformity with the Son, incarnate in Christ. It is an essential demand of the Christian life that we allow ourselves to be led by the spirit of God, the giver of all good gifts.

It is in this way that the kingdom of God will be established in us. This kingdom, the rule of God's love in men's hearts, is essentially a free gift of God. It is God, not we, who sets up his rule in the world. Our rôle is precisely to be ruled, which simply means to allow ourselves to be loved. The more we yield ourselves to God, the more we strive against our desire to be our own masters, the greater will be the advance of God's kingdom within us, and the more will we contribute to the progress of the Church, which is the visible and social expression of God's kingdom here on earth.

A HOLY PEOPLE

We pass now to another characteristic feature of the people of God. It is called to be a holy people. Its vocation is to separate itself from the world and cleave to God, for that is the meaning of holiness. The obligation to holiness is clearly stated by Yahweh to the Israelites; it is an inescapable consequence of their choice as his people. 'You shall be holy, for I the Lord your God am holy.' [7] The New Testament restates this obligation for Christians, and St Paul, by quoting the Old Testament, clearly underlines the continuity between the old and the new people in respect of this demand. 'For we are the temple of the living God; as God said: I will live in them and move among them, and I will be their God, and they shall be my people. Therefore come out of them, and be separate from them, says the Lord, and touch nothing unclean: then I will welcome you.' [8] And in the Epistle to the Hebrews the clear warning is given: 'Strive for peace with all men and for that holiness without

[7] *Lev.* 19: 2.
[8] 2 *Cor.* 6: 16.

which no one will see the Lord.'[9] It is clear from these texts that the very idea of a people specially chosen by God includes the notion of holiness. The effect of God's call is to summon this people out of the sinful world, to separate them from the mass of sinners and draw them close to himself, who is the All-holy.

Applying this to the Christian life, we see immediately that the Christian, by the very fact of his calling, is bound to be holy. We see too what this involves: negatively, conversion from the world and from self, a constant separating from what is not God; positively, a whole-hearted turning towards God and search for union with him. In this way the theocentric character of Christian holiness emerges clearly. The aim is not primarily to perfect ourselves but to seek God, to draw near to him and in doing so to become the kind of person he wants us to be, to become in fact like him. To be holy is to make God the goal and centre of our lives, to serve him with all our strength and in every possible way. God looks therefore for observance of his commands, whether they concern ethical duties or cultual observances. He looks too for interior homage, without which all outward conformity is an abomination to him. And he desires that through this service his goodness and his power should be made known before the world—as we read in *Isaiah*, 'the people whom I formed for myself, that they might declare my praise';[10] and as we find too in the famous passage of 1 *Peter* on the royal priesthood of Christians, 'But you are a chosen race, a royal priesthood, a holy nation, God's own people, that you may declare the wonderful deeds of him who called you out of darkness into his marvellous light.'[11]

It is then a rich and many-sided service that God demands of his people. Looking at it more closely we see that it has two general aspects: a complete transformation of the personality, through growing likeness to God; and, on the other hand,

[9] *Heb.* 12: 14.
[10] *Is.* 43: 21.
[11] 1 *Peter* 2: 9.

witnessing to God before one's fellow-men. We might express the two together in the theological idea of God's glory, that is, God's infinite majesty and goodness as shown forth in creation. We are called to share in that infinite goodness by becoming like to God, and in this way the glory of God is extended objectively in God's giving of himself to us. We are called too to acknowledge God's goodness and make it known to others, and in this way the glory of God is extended subjectively in the minds of men. Thus the Christian vocation to holiness may be adequately described as a service devoted to God's glory. In this light too we can more readily appreciate the force of St Peter's reference to the royal priesthood in the passage quoted above. From the beginning the priestly dignity and function of the people of God had been clearly stated. In the *Exodus* we read, 'You shall be my own possession among all peoples; for all the earth is mine, and you shall be to me a kingdom of priests and a holy nation.' [12] It is no doubt this passage that St Peter is echoing when he tells the Christians that they are 'a chosen race, a royal priesthood, a holy nation, God's own people.' One is struck in these texts by the close connection between the idea of priesthood on the one hand and that of holiness and belonging to God on the other. The explanation of the association is in fact quite simple, for the function of priesthood is to effect union with God; and sacrifice, which is the characteristic priestly act, is, in the celebrated definition of St Augustine, 'every work tending to effect our beatitude by a holy union with God.' [13] A priestly people is therefore a holy people and vice versa, a people committed to the glory of God in the sense I have explained, to making God more effectively present in and among men and to having his praises sung because he is so great and good. Without going into any details about the precise priestly functions of the new people of God, perhaps enough has been said to show how central these functions are in the Christian life. To live the Christian life is essentially to be a worshipper of God. The whole Christian life

[12] *Exod.* 19: 5 f.
[13] *De Civitate Dei*, 10, 6, CSEL.

is a life of worship, and the Christian is called all the time to offer what the New Testament calls spiritual sacrifices,[14] a phrase which in biblical language means true, genuine, acceptable sacrifices, sacrifices offered in the spirit of true worship. It is easy to see how central the liturgy must be in such a life, for even though every good action is a true sacrifice, it is in the liturgy that worship and sacrifice reach their highest expression and culmination.

But how is it possible for sinful men to draw near to God? How can they become like to God and so offer him the true worship of a holy, priestly people? They can do so only through union with Christ, the great high-priest, the holy one of God. It is Christ alone who can give acceptable worship to the Father and extend his glory. Again, we find that the people of God becomes a reality only through being constituted in the body of Christ. As members of Christ Christians share in his holiness and so become God's holy people. By baptism, which incorporates them into Christ, they are separated from the world and consecrated to God, rescued from sin and given a share in God's life, which exists in its fullness in Christ. This is how God's objective glory, his infinitely perfect goodness is spread abroad; it is God's self-giving to the whole Christ, to the head first and then to the members because of their union with the head. As a result they are enabled to serve God in the ways that he desires: interior love and homage, observance of his commandments and performance of his cult. Further, they are able to praise his name and make it known to men; indeed this is achieved mainly by the very fact of living a holy life. ' So let your light shine before men,' says Christ, ' that they may see your good works and give glory to your Father who is in heaven.' [15] This is the subjective glory of which I spoke above, the declaring of God's praise. Of course it is Christ and Christ alone who has made known the Father's glory. His whole life was a manifestation of the Father's goodness, holiness and love, culminating in the supreme

[14] Cf. 1 *Peter* 2: 5, *Rom.* 12: 1, *Phil.* 4: 18, *Heb.* 13: 15 f.
[15] *Matt.* 5: 16.

witness of the cross; and it is only through union with him that the people of God can in turn bear witness to the Father.

In Christ then God has made for himself a holy people, which we are. To live the life of Christ is to live a holy life, a life marked by a constant turning from sin and a determined search for God. It is a life of joyous worship, the service of a priestly people totally dedicated to the glory of the Father.

And now we come again to the rôle of the Holy Spirit, through whom Christ operates all things in his body. Certainly, where holiness is concerned, it is not surprising to find that the power of the spirit of holiness is at work. A holy people must be fashioned by the Holy Spirit of God. As the spirit of love, he is holy, for love unites to God and it is in union with God that holiness consists. We are a holy people because the spirit of love dwells amongst us, thus making God present in our midst. 'For we are the temple of the living God,' says St Paul: 'as God said: I will live in them and move among them, and I will be their God, and they shall be my people.' [16] There is no time here to develop this theology of the temple of God or, more strictly, of the Holy Spirit. But it is easy to see, at least, that the temple of God is the place where God gives himself to men, and where men in turn render God the worship that is his due. The temple, in other words, is the 'holy place,' where union between God and man is effected, where a priestly people offers to God acceptable sacrifices. We are this temple and it is the presence of the Holy Spirit amongst us that makes us so. It is through him that God gives himself to us, and it is through him that our worship is carried to the Father. We saw already that the Holy Spirit is our constant benefactor and guide; now we see that he is the bond of holiness. Indeed by whatever road we should choose to approach the mystery of the Church in its relation to the Christian life, we should find ourselves led to the rôle of the Holy Spirit.

Before passing from this notion of a holy people let us look

[16] 2 *Cor.* 6: 16.

briefly at its relation to the kingdom of God. It is not difficult to see how the formation of a holy people serves to establish the kingdom. For a holy people is one that turns away from sin, thus fulfilling the primary requisite for the kingdom, which is conversion. 'Do penance,' says Christ, that is, turn away from sin, 'for the kingdom of God is at hand.'[17] Further, a holy people is one in which God's love reigns and his will is accomplished. It is one too in which his praises are sung, that is to say, in which his power and goodness are acknowledged and made known to men. The ideas of holiness and of the rule of God over men's hearts are therefore complementary and mutually illuminating. The holier we become, the more we advance God's kingdom. The more fully we submit ourselves to God's rule, the more we grow in holiness. An important factor in both conceptions is that the central rôle of God in the Christian life is well safeguarded, the will of God being clearly seen as the guiding principle of human life.

A COMMUNITY CALL

The third element in the notion of the people of God whose moral implications I should like to indicate is a very obvious one. It is the simple fact that it is a people, and not individuals, that God has called. A principle of unity and interdependence lies at the very root of our vocation. It follows that an individualist morality has no place in God's plan. As a Christian I have to face this astounding truth: concern with my own salvation is valid only insofar as I see myself as a member of God's people, for it is to this people that the call to salvation has primarily been given. It is indeed a personal call that I have received and my personality is not subordinated to the good of the community, as it would be in a collectivist society. There is rather a fruitful exchange between the individual and the community, in which the individual sees himself precisely as a member of the community, while the community safeguards and sustains the

[17] *Matt.* 4: 17.

individual. The community looks to the individual to enrich it with his own contribution to the common good, and so the moral life of the Christian must be inspired by the desire to confer the maximum service on his brethren. However, the service he is called to give is precisely his personal service. It is unique and irreplaceable and increases in value in proportion to his personal gifts and spiritual development. So far is the obligation to the community from stifling personal development, therefore, that it is in fact its safeguard and stimulus.

We find here then two very important principles of the Christian moral life: on the one hand, its corporate character, which forbids me to think of myself alone or indeed to rate my own spiritual good as in itself of more importance than that of others, although of course my responsibility for it is greater, since I have more control over it; on the other hand, the personal, or what may be called the existential character of the Christian life, which obliges me to develop to the full my own particular gifts, to co-operate with my own special graces, to seize upon the historical opportunities which present themselves to me and not to be satisfied simply with fulfilling general laws and clearly defined duties.

This line of thought is borne out in a striking way by the doctrine of the body of Christ. It is as members of this body that we are called by God. Each one of us is loved by God because we are joined to Christ and made one corporate person in him. It is the whole Christ that God has chosen. The individual Christian must therefore never lose sight of the good of the entire body and must find his own development in the service of the common good. Each has his part to play for the good of the whole body; and to refuse that service is to reject one's Christian calling. The image of the human body makes this quite clear, as St Paul shows in *Romans* and 1 *Corinthians*. Each member has meaning only in the context of the entire body and its welfare. On the other hand, it is precisely the particular service of each individual organ that the body needs; and what one gives cannot be given by another; what he does not give cannot be supplied. Christ looks to every member to fulfil his own unique rôle to the fullest possible measure.[18]

The principle which effects this unity in diversity, this personal development in a community context, is of course the one spirit of the body of Christ. Because all the members are vivified by the one spirit, their energies are directed towards the good of the whole body and harmoniously co-ordinated in mutual service.[19] One cannot remain under the influence of the spirit except by concerning oneself with the welfare of one's fellow members. On the other hand, it is precisely the spirit of Christ that enables the individual to reach his true personal development, to realize his latent powers of nature and grace by yielding himself more and more to the love of God. The spirit is the true source of originality and freedom, of authentic personal fulfilment, and it is precisely by fostering these values that he provides for the good of the entire body.

The relevance of all this to the establishment of the kingdom of God is easily seen. If this kingdom operates primarily in the hearts of men, where it becomes a principle of personal freedom and development, it is also destined to be a kingdom in a visible and social sense. The rule of God in the universe is directed to the establishment of a unified and ordered community, of which the Church militant is in fact the earthly realization. Without a corporate consciousness and a spirit of mutual service no such kingdom could continue to exist. If we wish to let God rule in our hearts, therefore, we must have a care for the order and welfare of the entire community. It must be our concern to avoid dissensions and divisions, and to foster the unity of the Church by prayer, example and suitable activity.

THE LAW OF GOD'S PEOPLE

The fourth and last feature of the people of God I have selected for treatment, is the law by which this people is constituted. On Mount Sinai God gave the law to Moses, thereby providing

[18] *Rom.* 12: 4–8; 1 *Cor.* 12.

[19] 1 *Cor.* 12: 4–13.

a constitution and a way of life for the people he had called into existence. The law was the principle that ensured the union of the Israelites with God, for it brought them into conformity with his will. It also guaranteed unity and ordered social intercourse among the people, for it included not only general moral duties and cultural prescriptions, but also detailed rules for the regulation of social and political life and institutions. The goodness and value of the law are therefore beyond question. In itself, however, it did not give the power to observe its commandments. Moreover, it was exposed to the danger of a twofold corruption: the multiplication and over-stressing of minute legal rules, and, secondly, self-sufficiency and pride on the part of those who succeeded in observing it.

When Christ came, he did not reject the law. On the contrary he came to bring the law to perfection. As head of the new people of God, which is his body, he was a new Moses, proclaiming a law that reiterated all that was good in the old law, but went far beyond it. With great force he attacked the attitude of the Pharisees, who were guilty of the twofold distortion of the law which I have mentioned. To counter their errors he stressed the primacy of the central moral obligations of the law, justice, sincerity and mercy, and showed how the heart and essence of the law is love, from which all the individual obligations derive their value. Moreover, he himself gave, in his own life and death, the perfect example of the law he preached, thereby giving it a new clarity and force. Thirdly, and most importantly, he gave to the members of his body the power to observe the law, by giving them a share in the divine love which was the law of his own being, the driving force of his life. Again, we see that it is only in and through Christ that the people of God becomes a reality, only in becoming Christ's body that it can realize its vocation and fulfil the demands God makes on it. In the new people of God which is the body of Christ, law has not been abolished. The situation is radically changed, however, for law has now been introduced into the heart, where it moves men from within and unites them to God, giving the power to fulfil the external precepts and indeed to go beyond them in loving and joyful service.

But, of course, all this too takes place in the power of the Holy Spirit. It is the spirit of Christ who transmits to us Christ's law. At Pentecost the Holy Spirit came into the Church as the law of Christ's mystical body and of every individual member in it. It is he who introduces into our hearts the love of Christ, which is the principal element in the new law. It is he too who, through the Pope and the bishops, who are his instruments, teaches us the external precepts imposed by Christ. The Church's interpretation and application of these precepts, whether of the natural or divine positive law, is also the work of the Holy Spirit, in the sense that it rests on his authority and enjoys his guidance, in proportion, of course, to the source from which it emanates and the binding force with which it is imposed.

The prescriptions of Canon Law too, which seek to create the best conditions for the Christian life, can justly claim the authority of the Holy Spirit, despite the fact that a particular law may well be unnecessary or imprudent, or have outlived its usefulness. The complicated question of when, and by whom, a merely ecclesiastical law is to be adjudged devoid of force, is one which I have not the time, nor I fear, the competence to discuss. It is relevant to the problem, however, to remark that all ecclesiastical law derives its justification from the end which is it designed to serve, namely the good of souls, more concretely, their union with God in love. The Holy Spirit who lends his authority to ecclesiastical law is the spirit of love, whose sole purpose in the Church is to promote divine love in men's souls; it follows that Church laws must be inspired and informed by love and must from time to time be subject to revision to ensure that they truly promote the work of love. Nor should it be forgotten in making this revision that laws may be harmful for the sole reason that they are too numerous, thus tending to obscure the primacy of charity and the true proportions of Christian moral teaching. It is important too that the law-makers be conscious of the great variety of human circumstances and of the different paths by which the Holy Spirit, who is the spirit of freedom and diversity as well as of unity, leads men to union with God. If they bear this in mind they will recognize that Canon Law, to be truly useful, must possess a certain elasticity or adaptability, which will enable it to reduce to a minimum any conflict between the law and the individual conscience, for which the final law is the interior guidance of the Holy Spirit. Catholic theology does indeed dispose of a number of principles which which can give to Canon Law the flexibility it needs. They have not, unfortunately, always received the attention they deserve, nor have they always been properly understood. I refer to such concepts as equity, custom, *epikeia*, recourse to the legislator, dispensation, excusation, privilege, toleration. A particular kind of canonist may tend to dismiss some, at any rate, of these notions with a smile, as not to be taken quite seriously, or perhaps with a frown, as likely to sow confusion and trouble. But a true understanding of the purpose of Canon Law will lead to a juster appreciation of their value. It is indeed only by according them their proper place that Canon Law can hope to retain the respect and prestige to which it is entitled, for otherwise it will inevitably appear harsh and unbending, unfitted for ruling a community whose highest law is the spirit of love.[20]

Having said so much, there is no need for me to linger on the contribution the new law has to make to establishing the kingdom of God. Every kingdom must have its law, and the kingdom of God is no exception. It is the function of the new law to establish the rule of God's love in men's hearts and, by its external precepts, to lay down the guide-lines within which this rule is intended to operate. It is its function too to unite the subjects of the kingdom in love with one another, and to safeguard the external relationships without which this love could not exist and thrive. To the extent that it is allowed to fulfil these functions —and of course a certain substantial measure of fulfilment is

[20] For a useful discussion of the true role of the juridical element in the Church see C. Kemmeren, O.F.M., *Ecclesia et Jus. Analysis Critica Operum Josephi Klein*, Rome, 1963, 121–35.

infallibly guaranteed—the law ensures to the kingdom a visible and corporate expression in which the complementary claims of liberty and law, spirit and letter, community and institution, diversity and unity are harmoniously satisfied, and in which the inexhaustible fecundity of the grace of Christ is revealed through the rich and varied life of the community of his spirit, the people of God which is his body.

THE MASS IN THE CHRISTIAN LIFE

Dermot Ryan

The Constitution on the Liturgy suggests a profitable method of relating the Mass to the Christian life when it says: ' The renewal in the Eucharist of the covenant between God and man draws the faithful into the compelling love of Christ and sets them on fire ' (par. 10). It would take us too far afield to discuss the implications of the word ' covenant ' in the Scriptures; but the meaning which is familiar to all of us, namely ' agreement,' will serve the purpose of this paper. We are then discussing the Mass ' as the renewal of the agreement between God and man.' This way of describing the theme may seem rather startling, especially when we recall that the gift of God's saving grace is purely gratuitous. The infinite superiority of God would seem to preclude the possibility of an agreement between God and man; it is for God to command, and for man to obey. A little reflection on the Scriptures, however, will reveal that the whole plan of salvation advances through a series of such covenants or agreements between God and man, and while the superior position of God is safeguarded, the terms of these agreements are clearly set out and accepted as binding both by God and man.

GOD'S COVENANT WITH HIS PEOPLE ISRAEL

In recent years scholars have devoted their attention to this use of the covenant to describe the relationship between God and his chosen people. They have examined ancient treaties concluded between nations surrounding Israel, and have found parallels to biblical covenants in the literary form, the wording and the accompanying ritual of these treaties. Since at least some of the treaties are earlier than the Patriarchs, it is clear that this ritual and form influenced the people of God when they came to formulate their relationship with Yahweh.

The covenant of God with Noah shows God imposing on himself the obligation never again to destroy all flesh by flood waters. The making of the covenant appears in two forms: in the first (*Gen.* 8: 20–22) it is linked with the offering and acceptance of Noah's sacrifice; in the second the sign of the covenant is the rainbow: 'When the bow is seen in the clouds, I will remember my (v. 16 everlasting) covenant . . . and the waters shall never again become a flood to destroy all flesh' (*Gen.* 9: 14–15). In each form of the covenant the obligations are clearly stated and are then ratified by a visible sign or symbol. It is true that Almighty God alone seems to bind himself by this agreement, but it must be remembered that Noah was already described as a 'just man' (*Gen.* 6: 8–9). Because he was a just man, God was able to enter into this bond of friendship with him. His justice and holiness meant that his heart was open to God, and God could communicate with him. The very first covenant of the Bible therefore stressed the need for moral uprightness in those entering a covenant relationship with God.

The ritual of the covenant between God and Abraham in *Genisis* 15 seems rather bewildering. Abraham is invited to cut certain animals in two and lay the halves on the ground opposite each other. In a dream he sees Yahweh pass between the pieces in the form of a burning brazier.

This ritual was used by men to bring home to the contracting parties the seriousness of their obligations. Their action in passing between the pieces of the animals was an invitation to the gods to punish them with the fate of the animals if they should fail to live up to the obligations arising from the covenant. Abraham was, therefore, made aware of God's firm intention to give Palestine to his descendants. God bound himself by the most solemn covenant ritual known to the men of the time, and Abraham could be sure he would be faithful.

This covenant is also set in the context of Abraham's obedience to God's commands (*Gen.* 12: 4), while his faith makes him just in the eyes of God (*Gen.* 15: 6).

The same emphasis is found in the introduction to the account of the circumcision covenant in *Genesis* 17: 'I am God Almighty; walk before me and be blameless and I will make my covenant between me and you' (*Gen.* 17: 1–2). Circumcision was the permanent sign of this covenant and expressed the idea of consecration to the service of Yahweh as a member of his chosen people with a corresponding right to share in its inheritance.

The covenant at Sinai is described in much greater detail as befits the event which saw the birth of Israel as the people of God. Only those elements can now be considered which are relevant to the theme under discussion.

Yahweh identifies himself as the saviour of his people: 'I am Yahweh, your God, who brought you out of the land of Egypt' (*Exod.* 20: 2; cf. 19: 4–6). He has done enough for his people to make them aware of his love. His efforts on their behalf surely merit a response. In the laws which follow, the Israelites learn the pattern of this response. They are left in no doubt about the terms of their loving service. When it came to the formal ratification of this covenant, Moses read 'the book of the covenant' which contained these laws, and the people said: 'All that Yahweh has spoken we will do, and we will be obedient' (*Exod.* 24: 7).

The present text of *Exodus* has gathered together a number of traditions concerning the ritual of ratification of the Sinaitic covenant. The various rites serve to emphasize different aspects of this covenant between God and man.

The pillars of stone (*Ibid.* 24: 4) which were firmly fixed in the ground, would stand through the centuries to recall the making of the covenant at this place. The earliest examples of such treaty stones bore no text, which meant that their significance might easily be forgotten. As a result the practice was introduced of inscribing the terms of the treaty on such stone pillars. The Book of Exodus makes no reference to inscriptions on the pillars; but it does record the writing of the laws on the tablets of stone (*Exod.* 31: 18; 34: 1 ff.). This durable material would be a permanent record of the terms of the covenant. The book of the covenant was later placed beside the ark of the covenant (*Deut.* 31: 26). This recalls the practice of depositing treaty texts in the sanctuary so that the enforcement of their terms might be committed to the gods who were worshipped there. In the texts themselves these gods were invoked as witnesses and also as executors of curses and blessings which met failure or fidelity in fulfilling the terms of the agreement.

The sacrifices offered on the occasion of the making of the covenant are described as ' burnt offerings and peace offerings ' (*Ibid.* 24: 5). The term for peace offerings is closely connected with the Semitic word for peace (shalom, salaam, etc.) and it is worth noting that this latter term occurs frequently in the ancient treaties to describe the state of peaceful fellowship which should be shared by both parties as a result of the treaty. They, therefore, ' establish a certain community between God and Israel ' (McCarthy, *Treaty and Covenant*, 176). It is however the sprinkling of the blood of these sacrifices which most graphically expresses the union between Yahweh and his people. The blood was sprinkled on the altar representing Yahweh, and on the people. This ritual symbolically constituted a blood relationship between the contracting parties. Each, as it were, joined the family of the other, and was bound by family or tribal loyalty to honour the terms of the covenant. By sharing the same blood in the ritual Yahweh and the people became related by blood; Yahweh became the father of his people. From now he must have a father's care for his children. He must bless them in their enterprises and give them success; their crops and beasts must be fruitful; he must make them strong and prosperous. This prosperity and success were regarded as a share in God's own blessedness, a share in his life. In return for the privilege of his loving protection the people must give Yahweh devoted service, so that in every sense he could make them his own (cf. *Exod.* 19: 4 ff.).

While sprinkling the blood on the people Moses said: ' Behold the blood of the covenant which Yahweh has made with you in accordance with all these words ' (*Exod.* 24: 8). Although the blood of the covenant consecrates this relationship between Yahweh and his people, attention is drawn to the terms of this relationship by the phrase: 'in accordance with all these words.' The relationship symbolized by the sharing of the blood can be experienced in its fullness only if due regard is had for the terms of service expressed in the laws to which the people had promised obedience.

When peace offerings were made to God, it was customary to return part of the animal to the worshippers so that they might partake of a sacrificial meal. The animal had already been offered to God and had been accepted by him; it now belonged to him. By restoring part of it for a sacrificial meal, he was equivalently inviting his worshippers to join him in eating a meal, to join the family circle, as it were. This was a well recognized method of concluding an agreement amongst the Semites (cf. for example, *Gen.* 31: 54), and is reflected in the phrase ' to eat salt with ' which could mean ' to make an agreement with.' It is in this context that one must read *Exodus* 24: 11, where it is said of Moses and the elders on the mountain: ' They beheld God, and ate and drank.' Although this passage may derive from a different source from *Exodus* 24: 5–8, its inclusion in the text in its present position is intended to suggest that the covenant ritual concluded with a covenant meal. This was an expression of friendship and common purpose between God and the chosen representatives of his people.

Once the basic relationship between Yahweh and his people had been established by word and sacrifice, Israel was invited to set up a permanent sign of the abiding presence of God in her midst, namely the ark of the covenant. This sacred chest contained objects which were associated with Israel's deliverance from Egypt (for example, Aaron's rod, manna) which made

Israel aware of Yahweh's loving interest in her. It also contained the decalogue inscribed on stone tablets (*Deut.* 10: 1–5), a permanent reminder of the terms under which Yahweh's loving relationship with Israel might continue. The top of the ark bore the figures of cherubim on which Yahweh sat enthroned. It was therefore at the ark that the presence of Yahweh among his people was localized. It was to the ark that they came to worship their God, and to implore his help in time of need.

The memory of this covenant was never let die in the tradition of Israel. At times it was dimmed when Israel was distracted by the lure of wealth or the hope of power, and tried to substitute these earthly props for the sustaining hand of God. Bitter experience made them aware of their error, and the outcome showed that their basic instincts which were derived from the covenant, always remained sound. They knew that their failure was unfaithfulness to the covenant, so they returned in sorrow to their forgotten God and renewed their covenant with him.

Joshua 24 is a clear example of this renewal of the covenant, and reproduces many features of the ancient covenant forms. Yahweh presents himself in the historical introduction (*Ibid.* 2–13), and recalls his generous treatment of his people in the time of the Patriarchs, in Egypt, at Sinai, and finally in the Promised Land. He now asks them once for all to ' put away the gods which your fathers served beyond the river ' (*Ibid.* 14). The people responded: ' Far be it from us that we should forsake Yahweh to serve other gods ' (*Ibid.* 16). Joshua recorded their words in a book, and a great stone was set up at the sanctuary of Yahweh to recall the people's renewed determination to serve their God.

At the end of the eighth century B.C., king Hezekiah succeeded Ahaz who, under pressure from Assyria, had introduced pagan worship to the Temple at Jerusalem. Under Hezekiah's leadership the people disowned his conduct, and when the Temple had been purified, they offered sacrifices for sin before renewing the covenant to the accompaniment of peace offerings (cf. 2 *Kings* 18: 1–8; 2 *Chron.* 29). This case of renewal is instructive because it shows that the basic relationship established by the covenant at Sinai continued in spite of the infidelity of the people. It was only because this relationship continued that they were in a position to offer the sacrifices for sin prescribed by the law for the people of the covenant. It was only because these sacrifices were offered in sorrow by the people of the covenant that they were acceptable to God. There was therefore a 'once for all time' element in the events at Sinai, which could never be disturbed by the people's failure, and required no renewal. The people required frequent reminders of their covenant obligations and frequent opportunities to renew their determination to be faithful. These helps to fidelity were given in the cult. Although it is not certain that a special feast was set aside for the renewal of the covenant, all the great feasts implied such a renewal in so far as they were prescribed by the law, and were carried out by the people of Yahweh to do honour to their covenant God. The sacrifices of individuals had a similar significance in the individual case, and the sin offerings prescribed by the law could be regarded as restoring to perfection the covenant relationship which had been blemished by sin.

An examination of the texts which record a renewal of the covenant (*Joshua* 24; 2 *Chron.* 29; 2 *Kings* 22 and 23; *Neh.* 9–12: 43) reveals the elements which were used on such occasions. Not all of them are found in each case, but the overall pattern is similar. They may be listed as follows:

1. Acknowledgement of failure to keep the terms of the covenant.
2. The decision to renew the covenant.
3. Preparatory purification. (This can be done because the basic covenant relationship still exists and the ritual used is therefore acceptable to the covenant God.)
4. A history—of varying length—of God's generosity and fidelity and the contrasting infidelity of the people.
5. Reading of the law. (The Hebrew word for law—torah—implies not only laws, but also instruction.)

6 Renewed acceptance of the God of the covenant and his terms; determination to obey.
7 A permanent record (for example, writing, stone pillars).
8 Sacrifices.
9 Sacrificial meal.

It is worth noting that in *Joshua* 24 there is no mention of sacrifice. But this does not necessarily mean that no sacrificial rite accompanied the renewal of the covenant. In fact the link between covenant and sacrifice in Hebrew tradition is very strong: 'Gather to me my faithful ones, who made a covenant with me by sacrifice' (*Ps.* 50: 8).

The Israelites made the ancient treaty-form their own; but because the covenant or agreement was between God and man and not between two earthly kings, they modified it by attributing a most important role to the mediator of the covenant, who had rarely appeared in the ancient treaties.

The Israelites also broke away from the excessively legal language and form of these ancient treaties. Their elaboration of certain treaty elements was oratorical in character, and served as an exhortation to fidelity. The Book of Deuteronomy has the historical introduction, the laws, the covenant ritual, and the curses and blessings of the ancient treaties. But the exhortations, explanations and warnings of Moses breathe the warmth of a religious fervour which will not be hampered by a legal form. This flexibility in the use of a covenant form continues into the New Testament, and is to be found in the arrangement of the Last Supper and the present form of the Mass.

In the covenants described above it was clear that the infinite dignity of Yahweh was in no way compromised by the covenant form. In each it was he who made the first move; it was he who laid down the stipulations which governed the relationship between himself and his people. The covenant ritual used on those occasions was a visible and symbolic manifestation of God's unfailing fidelity to his covenant promises.

The ritual described in these texts was taken from current

legal practice in concluding solemn agreements. It corresponds —very roughly—to the witnessed signature, the wax and the seals of our own legal system. If then the relationship between Yahweh and his people is expressed in a formula which is the common practice of a legal system, is there not a danger that the religion of Yahweh may be reduced to legalistic formalism? The fact that at times the religion of the Jews became excessively legalistic shows that the danger was inherent in the system, but the system also carried its own safeguards and correctives.

The first of these was the experience from which the relationship grew. The people of Israel who lived through the deliverance from Egypt and experienced the favours of Yahweh in the desert, knew that he was not an impersonal force to be manipulated by a ritual technique, but a person who rescued and saved his people because he loved them.

The second element which sets the tone of the relationship is the ritual which accompanied the making of the covenant. The sprinkling of the blood symbolized a blood relationship with Yahweh who became the father of his people, and the covenant meal conveyed an atmosphere of familial and familiar intimacy with the covenant God.

These elements of the covenant-making were, in a sense, proper to those who were present at Sinai, but even then they were not carried out in wordless mime. The declarations of Moses, the dialogue with the people and their determined response gave a meaning to their actions which could not be mistaken. To remove all shadow of doubt the words were carefully formulated and exactly recorded. Future generations should have no difficulty in sharing the experience of Sinai with the help of its words and its ritual, as we are reminded by the words of the Jewish Passover: 'Each one of us must think of himself as having passed out of Egypt.'

What was the nature of Yahweh, the covenant God? He manifested himself to the Israelites as personal, spiritual and one. In his spiritual personality he was utterly distinct from vague cosmic forces of a physical nature which were thought by many to control the universe. Being one, he was contrasted with the over-populated pantheons of the surrounding nations. Without the help of revelation these nations invented a god for every influence in the life and movement of the universe. They felt the need for a personal god, but the gods of the pantheon were a poor substitute. They lacked the freedom of personality and acted as they did only because they could not act otherwise. Instead of being persons, they were physical forces with personal names. Yahweh on the other hand was supremely free and in perfect control.

In his actions this personal, spiritual and one God revealed certain qualities which governed his relationship with his people and determined their attitude to him. He exercised his power on their behalf by delivering them from Egypt, and in the manner of his deliverance he showed that all creation was at his beck and call. The power of Yahweh the Saviour and Yahweh the Creator would always command the respect of his people. It was the basis for their religious awe at Sinai, but it also inspired confidence because it was at Israel's disposal in time of need.

When David and Jonathan concluded a covenant of love and affection, David expected that this relationship would be governed by the virtue of *hesed*, a word which is variously translated by loving kindness or mercy. It was frequently associated with *'emeth*, faithfulness, as being the characteristic virtues of the covenant relationship. Yahweh exercised these to perfection by a generous solicitude for his people which never failed: 'The faithfulness of Yahweh endures forever' (*Ps.* 117: 2), and *Psalm* 136 repeats the refrain: 'For his mercy endures forever.'

The righteousness or justice of Yahweh gave Israel assurance of just judgment and a court of appeal against any perversion of justice. Israel learned from experience that membership of the chosen people was no protection against the just judgment of God, and in the Psalms sinners appeal to God's justice tempered by mercy as a basis for forgiveness.

The description of the covenant as a relationship of love owes much to the experience and teaching of Hosea. For him Israel was the spouse of Yahweh to whom Yahweh was united by a passionate and tender love. The extent and the depth of this love can be measured by God's perseverance in it even when Israel had become a harlot and an adulteress. If Yahweh is angry at the unfaithful conduct of Israel, it is an expression of anguish at the rejection of his love rather than a wish to condemn and destroy. The love of the covenant God 'clearly demonstrates the inadequacy of all legal categories for the task of describing man's relationship with God' (Eichrodt, *Theology of the Old Testament*, I, 252).

God's anger was the reverse of his love or good pleasure and, in the covenant context, was the manifestation of his displeasure at some violation of the covenant terms. In contrast to his justice and loving kindness God's anger is not a permament feature of his relationship with Israel. It is never a blind or vengeful anger. It is a manifestation of displeasure which is intended to punish, but it is accompanied by the hope that it will effect a return.

The Old Testament's use of the concept of holiness is distinguished by the way in which it is linked with the person of Yahweh himself. He is the Holy One; all other persons, places and things are holy as a result of some divine activity, or because of their relation to the divinity. The priestly tradition conceived of God's holiness in terms of his complete otherness and absolute perfection in comparison with human beings and the cult was practised precisely in order to establish and maintain a link with the Lord. Many elements of the cult were common to other religions, but when taken over by the Hebrews, they acquired a deeper meaning. Yahweh himself had commanded that these rites should be practised, and in fulfilling his commands the worshippers had the assurance that they were doing God's will. With the handling and doing of holy things they were brought into the sphere of the divine.

With the preaching of the prophets greater emphasis is laid

on the moral aspects of holiness. It is not sufficient that a man should be ritually clean when approaching his God; he must also have fulfilled his moral obligations (cf. *Ps.* 15 and 24: 3–6). Yahweh could demand a ready obedience to his moral laws because moral perfection is what is essential to his holiness. When he says: 'You shall be holy; for I, Yahweh, your God am holy,' he is not referring merely to ritual and legal purity. If then Israel is admitted to the sphere of the divine, she can enter only if her conduct reflects the holiness of her God.

It would not be true to say that Israel was aware from the beginning of the nature of the covenant God in all its depth. Years of experience of Yahweh's care and the preaching of the prophets enriched their understanding of Yahweh. In his worship they found an outlet for every religious feeling and sentiment, as anyone who reads the Psalms can see. The majesty of an all-holy God did not exclude the intimate prayer of a child to his Father in heaven. The awe inspired by divine wrath did not silence the appeals for mercy and pardon. The glory of his works was chanted unceasingly and his goodness praised without end. Even a cursory reading of the Psalter shows convincingly that the relationship between Yahweh and his people could never be satisfied merely by the fulfilment of legal requirements. They were bound to one another by the bonds of affectionate love and not by a legal deed.

In spite of all these safeguards to ensure that the worship of Yahweh should never become a soulless technique performed according to the letter, and not the spirit of the law, the cult sometimes deteriorated to this level. People forgot the nature of the God they worshipped and ignored his moral demands. They performed the ritual prescribed by the law and disregarded the meaning it had in the law. They even thought that God should be content that it was done, and once their ritual obligations to him had been fulfilled, he would look with a benign eye on their worship of other gods.

THE NEW COVENANT

The people's failure provoked the anger of God with such frequency that, in the time of Jeremiah, he looked forward to the making of a new covenant, 'not like the covenant which I made with their fathers when I took them by the hand to lead them out of Egypt, my covenant which they broke . . . But this is the covenant which I will make with the house of Israel after those days, says Yahweh: I will put my law within them, and I will write it upon their hearts; and I will be their God and they shall be my people. And no longer shall each man teach his neighbour and each his brother, saying, Know Yahweh, for they shall all know me, from the least of them to the greatest, says Yahweh; for I will forgive their iniquity and I will remember their sin no more' (*Jer.* 31: 32–34).

Yahweh looks forward to the making of a covenant based on an interior and sincere knowledge of God which will be shared by all the people. An essential prerequisite for the establishment of such a covenant will be the forgiveness of sin.

Ezekiel also saw that sincerity would be a feature of the new covenant which through the influence of a new spirit would create a new heart in the people of Israel. For both Jeremiah (32: 40) and Ezekiel (16: 60) the new covenant is to be eternal.

In the second part of *Isaiah*, which is at least half a century later than the text of *Jeremiah*, we find the mysterious servant of Yahweh linked with the making of a covenant between Yahweh and his people:

'I have given you as a covenant to the people'
(*Isa.* 42: 6).

And in another passage it is said of him:

'By his knowledge shall the righteous one, my servant,
make many to be accounted righteous'
(*Isa.* 53: 11).

It is the same servant who would make himself an offering for sin (*Isa.* 53: 10) and bear the iniquity of all the people (*Ibid.* 53: 6) though he himself would be without sin (*Ibid.* 53: 9). This servant seems to be associated with the making of the covenant that is described in *Jeremiah*. He is equipped with a saving knowledge of Yahweh, and ensures abundant forgiveness of sins.

This was the expectation of the prophets immediately before and during the Exile; and if they hoped for a realization of the new covenant when the Exile would come to an end, their hopes were not realized in full. Shortly before the coming of Christ some Jews were well aware that these prophecies were still unfulfilled; and believing that the time for their fulfilment was near, they united in groups to prepare themselves as the nucleus of the people of the new covenant. Some groups of these Jews have left for us the writings we know as the Dead Sea Scrolls. It is not without interest that one fragment of these texts describes the work of the messianic king of *Isaiah* 11 in terms of kingdom and covenant:

> 'He will renew the covenant of the community
> and establish the kingdom of his people'
> (*Qumran Cave I*, Oxford, 1955, 127).

Christ preached his kingdom to his people and established it by sealing the new covenant in his blood.

It is rather surprising that apart from his words at the Last Supper the Evangelists do not record for us any statement of Christ which uses the word covenant. This word summed up the whole religion of the Old Testament, and it was a key theological term in the writings of *Qumran* which like *Jeremiah* and *Ezekiel* saw a covenant at the centre of God's 'new deal' for his people. One might therefore ask if the Gospel evidence implies that Christ made no use of this term in his preaching to the people. It may be that in his preaching he concentrated on the term 'kingdom' because it answered the popular expectation, and only used the term 'covenant' in what one might call the priestly or liturgical context of the Last Supper.

If this is what happened, it does not seriously affect our understanding of the Gospel, since from the time of King David onwards, kingdom and covenant were more and more closely identified. Evidence for this identification about the time of

Christ is provided by the passage from the *Qumran* text (quoted above) which puts kingdom and covenant in parallelism, and seems to regard them as equivalents.

The Sermon on the Mount displays quite clearly the role of Christ as mediator of a new law which would govern the relationship between God and his people, but even there, no specific mention is made of 'covenant.' The word appears for the first time on the lips of Christ when he gives to the apostles the rite by which the covenant in his blood could be renewed to the end of time. It is to this rite and its accompanying words that our attention is now drawn.

The words spoken by Christ over the chalice are our immediate concern. They occur in slightly varying forms, but the meaning is the same in each case. Christ points to the chalice and says that it contains his blood and he immediately links this blood with a new covenant. He goes on to say that this same blood will be shed for the apostles and for many for the remission of sins. We can see straight away how a number of the themes associated with the new covenant in both *Jeremiah* and *Deutero-Isaiah* come together in these words of Christ. We must therefore study them in their context.

Scholars continue to discuss whether the Last Supper was a paschal meal or not. There is abundant evidence for the view that it was, although some insoluble difficulties remain in this viewpoint. In any event the whole atmosphere of the Last Supper is that of a paschal meal, and the early Christians understood the Eucharist as the new pasch. In 1 *Corinthians* 5: 7 Christ is referred to as 'our pasch.' Then in 1 *Corinthians* 11: 26 St Paul says 'that as often as you eat this bread and drink the cup, you proclaim the Lord's death until he comes.' This implies that the eating of the bread of the Eucharist and the drinking of the Eucharistic wine proclaims the death of Christ, the new pasch. It also recalls the fact that his own death occurred in the context of the Passover feast of the Jews. There is therefore sufficient evidence for the paschal context in the Gospels and in the topographical and temporal setting of the death of Christ to provide an Exodus setting for the words of Christ over the chalice. The old covenant was established with the people of Israel during their journey from Egypt into the Promised Land. A new covenant would be established on the occasion of a new pasch, a new exodus from slavery. This time it is a going forth from the slavery of sin, a final deliverance into eternal happiness.

Following the pattern of the paschal meal prescribed by the Jewish law, Christ who presided over the group of the apostles would have recounted the wonderful works of God as recorded by the history of the Jews. He was required to do so by the law of *Exodus* 12: 26–7, which prescribed that an explanation of the paschal meal should be given by the head of the household. In the time of Christ the Passover meal was sometimes eaten by a group of disciples with their teacher. It was the teacher who then took the place of the head of the family and explained the meaning of the feast.

We are also told that Christ blessed (eulogesas) and gave thanks (eucharistesas). It was the custom among the Jews for the head of the household to bless and give thanks at all meals, but a particularly solemn and lengthy blessing and act of thanksgiving (for the Jews to bless and praise God was to thank him) accompanied the third cup of the paschal ritual. The traditional rites accompanying the meal therefore gave Christ at least two opportunities for explaining the significance of his work in the context of the history of salvation.

Christ's exposition of the benefits conferred on the Jewish people by their covenant with God, could well have followed the traditional pattern up to his own time. His own work made the addition of another chapter essential. God had now made a further revelation of himself in the person of his only-begotten Son and had called on men to enter into a new and fuller relationship with him.

The Synoptic Gospels do little more than hint that Christ spoke at some length at the Last Supper. Besides using the terms 'blessed' and 'gave thanks,' Matthew and Mark note how the going of the Son of man is linked with the fulfilment of Scripture. 'The Son of Man goes as it is written of him' (*Matt.* 26: 24). This may well conceal a longer explanation of his work in terms of Old Testament prophecy (cf. *Luke* 24: 25–27).

Luke 22: 14 recalls Christ's eagerness to eat this Passover before he suffered, an eagerness which obviously required some explanation to lift the gloom of impending disaster from the little group.

The Gospel of St John gives a lengthy discourse of our Lord at the Last Supper in which he spoke about his work, about the Father who had sent him, about the new law of love, about the coming of the Holy Spirit and about his going to prepare a place for all in the Promised Land (cf. *John* 14, 15, 16, 17).

When taken in conjunction with the brief references in the Synoptics, these texts show how the words of Christ at the Last Supper were a suitable preparation for the ritual conclusion of a new covenant. They spoke of the new revelation of the Father in the person of his Son, of the new life of union with God to which men were called. This new life must be governed by the new law of love and be directed by the Holy Spirit. The reward for faithful service in the new covenant was life with God in the new Promised Land. Christ as mediator concluded this covenant on man's behalf with his eternal Father and sealed it with his blood on Calvary. At the Last Supper he gave to men a sacrificial rite by which they could renew the making of this covenant and publicly assert their allegiance to it.

When Christ spoke of his blood in the words that he said over the chalice, he was referring to his sacrificial blood. The participle which goes with the word blood in the text of the Gospel is a present participle, but it may equally well be translated by the future. Christ therefore drew attention to the fact that this blood which was in the chalice was the blood which shall be shed for the remission of sins. The author of the Epistle to the Hebrews provides a ready commentary on these words of Christ in *Hebrews* 9: 22 he says that without the shedding of blood there is no forgiveness of sins, and he states quite clearly in the same chapter in verses 11 and 14 the immense value of the sacrificial blood of Christ when compared with the sacrificial blood of goats and bulls which was used in the Old Testament for the purification of the flesh. The blood of Christ, the Son of God, would be much more effective than the blood of the animals whose power was limited to the purifying of the body. The blood of Christ ' who through the eternal Spirit offered himself without blemish to God,' would purify the conscience of men from dead works to serve the living God (*Heb.* 8: 14).

This sacrificial blood is linked by Christ himself with a covenant. The very form of the words recalls what Moses said when he sprinkled the blood of the old covenant on the people and on the altar. Christ obviously wished to imply that just as the old covenant had been consecrated, sealed and signed in the blood of animals, so this new covenant was being consecrated, sealed and signed in his own precious blood. This was the new covenant promised by the prophets from Jeremiah onwards. They had looked forward to an improvement on the old covenant, especially in the abundance of knowledge of God and in the generous forgiveness of sins.

The new law governing this covenant is the law of love mentioned by Christ in the Gospel of St John. Something of the kind was given already in the Sermon on the Mount, where Christ clearly intended to alter and enlarge the commandments of the covenant at Sinai. These laws must now be re-interpreted in terms of the overall commandment to love God and one's neighbour.

For the author of *Hebrews* this covenant of Christ is more excellent than the old one by reason of the better promises on which it is enacted (8: 6). Christ has come to prepare a new Promised Land, to show us the way there and to give the food and the drink that men need to bear the rigours of this long and arduous journey. *Hebrews* also draws attention to the fact that it is a superior covenant, because it is consecrated by a more perfect sacrifice and by the blood of God the Son made man. Christ the victim continues to present himself with his blood and his wounds to plead unceasingly for us before the throne of his Father.

In view of the prophecy of *Jeremiah* (31: 34) special emphasis should be laid on the new knowledge of God which Christ shared with men and wished that all men should share. Christ knows God in the intimacy of his life, in the bosom of the Father; and it is this life that he reveals to us in becoming man: 'No one has ever seen God; the only Son who is in the bosom of the Father, he has made him known' (*John* 1: 18). 'He that sees me, sees the Father' (*Ibid.* 14: 9). It is this life too that he invites us to share. He is able to present God to men with such clarity, such authority, and such impact that he can make even greater demands on their generosity. The old covenant was established between Israel and the God who revealed himself as the Saviour of his people and Father of the children of Israel. It was because of what he had done for them, and because of this relationship by which he bound himself to them, that he expected a loving response. Christ now comes with a fuller knowledge and a fuller revelation and offering better promises to the children of God. He still expects a response in proportion to the generosity of the Father and he presents it to them in the terms of the commandment of love which they must show both to their God and to their neighbour.

The transition from the Last Supper to the Holy Sacrifice of the Mass is found in the words of Christ; 'Do this in memory of me.' We are reminded straight away of the frequent occasions in the Old Testament when the covenant of Sinai was recalled. A rite which resembled the original covenant ritual was used to recall the event and the obligations that were readily accepted on that occasion. This covenant renewal had the purpose of continuing, strengthening, developing and sometimes restoring to its fullness the covenant relationship between God and his people. On the occasion of these renewal ceremonies the people were given another opportunity to associate themselves with the covenant made in their name by Moses at Mount Sinai. Just as they inherited the hope and the promises which had been given to their ancestors, so they also inherited the responsibility to answer generously God's own generosity. Offering sacrifice to honour the God of the covenant, or to restore the relationship damaged by sin, or to participate in covenant renewal ceremonies, was to make use of the opportunity provided by God to associate themselves once again, publicly, with the covenant made in their name by Moses.

Christ seems to have something similar in mind when he asks that what he did at the Last Supper should be repeated by the apostles in memory of him. What precisely do these words mean: in memory of me? Scholars take the view that they mean primarily that Christ should be remembered favourably by God, in other words, that God by continually remembering the work of Christ would make it prosper. A project which was forgotten by God withered away and died; but if God remembered it, it prospered and met with success.

As we carry out these words of Christ uttered at the Last Supper and ask God to remember Christ and his work and to bless it, we are reminded that we too are associated with the success of this work, and we can participate in it and contribute towards it. We have only to think of the Old Testament to realize how the Israelites could impede the work of God by their failure to co-operate with the graces that God gave them. They could further his designs for men by seeking to live in accordance with the letter and the spirit of the law. As we now pray for the success of Christ's work and the establishment of God's kingdom on earth, we are also accepting the fact that we can contribute something towards the realization of this plan.

We are reminded of this too by the words which St Paul uses in reference to the Eucharist in the eleventh chapter of the First Epistle to the Corinthians. He said: 'As often as you eat this bread and drink the cup, you proclaim the Lord's death until he comes' (v. 26). Once again the Lord's death implies all that Christ is and was, and includes the whole work of redemption which he came to accomplish. The proclamation of the death of the Lord by us as we celebrate the Eucharist, is a proclamation which benefits, or is intended to benefit, not only those who are present, but all mankind. We associate ourselves with the cause for which Christ died; we wish to contribute to the completion of his plan, and by acting publicly we draw the attention of all mankind to the position we have taken. If their attention is focused on us in our daily lives, then they should get a clear impression that we really are contributing to the growth of the kingdom of God on earth. Our announcing of the death of the Lord should not be a purely ritual act; it involves the living of a Christian life amongst our fellow men outside the four walls of the Church. When St Paul says ' until he (the Lord) comes,' he relates the death of Christ and therefore his work of redemption to the final coming of Christ when this work shall be complete. This announcing of his death, this making known of the work that he had come to do, must continue until his plan has been perfectly completed. It is to the completion of this plan that we can contribute especially by a proper understanding and a proper use of the Holy Sacrifice of the Mass.

THE MASS AS COVENANT SACRIFICE

Our study of the Old Testament texts which are concerned with covenant making, and our re-reading of the account of the Last Supper in the light of those texts, lead us to the conclusion that in the Mass we have the elements of a covenant sacrifice. It is related to the covenant sacrifice of Calvary in a way which resembles that of the sacrifices of the Old Law in their relation to the covenant sacrifice at Mount Sinai. When the covenant was sealed at Mount Sinai, the Israelites were given the means for renewing the event in the sacrifices of the law. When Christ died on Calvary, sealing the covenant in his own precious blood, he had already given to his Church the means for re-presenting the sacrifice of the cross. The Mass surpasses the sacrifices of the law in the dignity of the victim who is present and in the effectiveness of his intercession as a mediator. It surpasses them too in the gift of the divine presence which it mediates in such an effective way, and in the divine food and drink which God shares with the people of the new covenant. It is, however, worth looking at the structure of the Mass in the light of what we have been saying about the making and the renewal of covenants in the Old Testament.

The first part of the Mass consists mainly of readings from the Old and the New Testaments, and they correspond to the first part of the covenant forms which we have examined in the Old Testament. They show God presenting himself to man under various aspects, and they record his dealings with man. In each intervention in history he makes known to man some new facet of his goodness, of his mercy, of his faithfulness, of his almighty power. This history culminates in the coming of Christ who is the full revelation of the Father in human terms. With a mingling of these readings from the Old and the New Testaments one is given a clear picture of the God of the covenant, old and new, the God who wishes to establish a special relationship with mankind, and has invited each one of us to associate ourselves with this covenant. Besides making known to us the kind of covenant God we worship, these texts make clear what God requires of his covenant people. We learn from the history of salvation who God is, and what we can expect God to do for us; we also learn from these readings what God expects us to do for him. We read, for example, in our missals passages of Scripture which remind us of the ten commandments, of the preaching of the prophets on justice and charity and sincerity in worship. St Paul can list for us the vices which exclude from the kingdom of heaven and the virtues which make us pleasing to God, while the words of Christ in the Gospel often invite us 'to go and do likewise' when we leave the church.

The chants of the Mass are often drawn from the Psalms, the book of prayers and songs to the covenant God. The fact that these prayers were originally uttered to the God of the old covenant and that they are now used in the worship of the God of the new, illustrates the continuity between the Old and the New Testaments. It is the same God revealing himself more fully in the New Testament who makes known to us his boundless generosity. Our response can find a ready expression in the words of the Psalms, from the abject fear of a sinner before the just anger of God, to the secure confidence of a child in his loving Father or the bounding joy of the creature rejoicing in the work of his Creator.

These readings of the Scriptures show us the God who loves us and how he loves us, and they tell us also how we should love God. The benefits that accrue to us because of our love of God have been mediated to us by Christ, who was God made man. He acted on our behalf, not in the sense that he was a substitute for us but that we are taken up into his person to form the whole Christ with him. It was he who by his death on the cross confirmed this covenant which he had made in our name with the eternal Father. It was because of the dignity of the person who suffered that his sacrifice was able to mediate a better covenant than the covenant of the old law. By giving us the sacrifice of the Mass at the Last Supper Christ made it possible for us to renew under the symbols of bread and wine the covenant sacrifice which was offered on Calvary. The separate consecration of the bread and wine represents the separation of body and blood which took place in such agony during the passion of Christ. We have then a sacrifice under signs which gives us an opportunity of renewing the original covenant sacrifice, and publicly associating ourselves with it.

In the second part of the Mass the actions which are performed would of themselves have little significance. They reproduce the core of the covenant sacrifice as instituted by Christ at the Last Supper and unfold their meaning through the words which accompany them. The words reach back into Old Testament times in recalling God's kindness to Israel. They repeat the words of Christ by which he once again becomes present as the covenant victim and they implore that our worthy conduct may win for us a share in his kingdom.

The Communion is reminiscent of the covenant meal which generally followed the offering of the covenant sacrifice. The gifts had been offered to God and favourably received by him, and had been consecrated by this reception. Through the priest, they were then handed back by God to those who were associated with him in this covenant. The worshippers were nourished with a divine food, and were united in a covenant community with God and with one another. This practice of the Old Testament is fulfilled in an utterly unexpected way by the sacrament of the Eucharist in which the gift of himself by Christ is received by the eternal Father and given back to men who associate themselves with his covenant, with his work. By participation in the covenant of Christ they have begun to lead a divine life and to share in divine blessings. Great demands are made on them if they are to live up to the requirements of God's will. The standard of conduct which is demanded of those who are associated with the covenant of Christ far exceeds the demands of the old law as can be seen in the Sermon on the Mount. The weakness of men is unchanged and they could never reach the standards expected of them without help from God. This help was given through the food of the Eucharist, the covenant meal, which nourishes men with this divine food and equips them with the power of Christ himself: 'He that eats my flesh and drinks my blood abides in me and I in him' (*John* 6: 57). United in Christ, they are also united with one another.

A consequence of the sacrifice of the Mass which runs parallel to the Old Testament covenant is the abiding presence of Christ in the Blessed Sacrament. As a result of the covenant made on Sinai God dwelt amongst his people enthroned on the cherubim over the Ark. There the Israelites could commune with their covenant God. Since Christ is present in the Blessed Eucharist in the tabernacle, Christians can pray to him who is the mediator of the new covenant with the eternal Father, the mediator of the promises, the blessings and the helps which are associated with it. Just as the Israelites by praying at the tabernacle in the desert accepted the covenant and the relationship which it established between them and their God, so those who visit the Blessed Sacrament reserved in the tabernacle are associating themselves once more with the covenant made in their name by Christ, established by the covenant sacrifice on Calvary and frequently renewed by the covenant sacrifice of the Mass. From the tabernacle we can draw strength to live in accordance with the stipulations of this covenant, and we are reminded of the destiny of those who have shared the covenant meal with their Lord and their fellow Christians: 'He who eats my flesh and drinks my blood has life everlasting, and I will raise him up on the last day' (*John* 6: 55).

Our investigation has shown the continuity of the tradition in the Old and New Testaments which links the making of the covenant between God and man with the offering of sacrifice. In this context the Mass appears as the covenant sacrifice of the new law, a notion which has relevance for the title of this paper: 'The Mass in the Christian Life.' The living of the Christian life means living according to the stipulations of the new covenant made in our name by Christ with the eternal Father. When we go to Mass, we publicly associate ourselves with the act of Christ in making this covenant. With the help of the texts of the Mass we worship his eternal Father. We worship his eternal Father as made known to us by Christ; we believe in him; we accept his word; we become aware of his fidelity to his own promises; we become aware of the glorious blessings that await us if only we are faithful; we learn in detail of the demands which are made on us by God in accordance with the terms of the covenant. It is therefore made clear to us in the earlier part of the Mass why we have come into the church, what we have come to do, what are the consequences of what we do in the church. The real test of our sincerity in associating ourselves with the covenant sacrifice of Christ is the way we live the Christian life when we leave the church. It is true that the rite and the words have a peculiar sacredness by reason of the real presence of our Lord in the sacrament of the Eucharist. One should not however forget that in the Old Testament even those rites and those words which were consecrated in covenant usage, lost their meaning by unthinking repetition. It would be a pity if the same should happen to our attendance at the sacrifice of the Mass. The best protection against such a defect is careful attention to the Scripture readings of the Mass. In their richness of content and variety of emphasis they keep reminding us of what we are at when we offer the Holy Sacrifice.

The importance of the vernacular in the Mass as the covenant sacrifice is obvious. No one wishes to sign a document he has neither read nor understood. No one should be invited to associate himself with the pact that Christ has made in our name without a reminder of the nature of his commitment. When the Scriptures are read to us in intelligible language and are related in the homily to the circumstances of our daily lives, there can be no doubt about what we are committed to when we leave the church after Mass.

Since the Mass is a public and a social act we should be aware of the fact that we have publicly proclaimed our loyalty to the cause of Christ and the demands of Christ's love. Any conduct which falls short of the Christian ideal, is also a public denial of the word we have given in the name and the blood of Christ when last we assisted at Mass.

Any offence against our fellow Christians is particularly odious, since all have received the same divine gifts of the body and blood of Christ and live by his life. It is unseemly that rifts and quarrels should separate Christians who are associated in this sacred act, and are bound together by the sacred bonds of the covenant promise, sacrifice and meal.

Mere avoidance of strife with one's fellow worshippers is not the ideal of the Christian community. Since all have assembled around the altar of God and at the Communion table as children of one Father, they must share the sorrows and trials of their brothers and sisters in Christ. It is easy to share in joy and success; it is not so easy to lighten the load of sorrow which accompanies sickness and failure, disappointment and death. Yet no one in need in a Christian community should be without help. Christians could say of their attendance at Mass: 'We used to hold sweet converse together; within God's house we walked in fellowship' (*Ps.* 55: 14). It was never intended by Christ that this fellowship should be limited to the act of worship. It must extend beyond the walls of the church and embrace all those who are in need.

When the Mass is understood as the renewal of the covenant sacrifice, it is constantly related by its texts to the living of the Christian life. The sacrificial rite seals in the blood of Christ the determination of the faithful to live this life. Communion unites them in a common life and a common source of strength. No wonder that the Constitution on the Liturgy says that 'the renewal in the Eucharist of the covenant between God and man draws the faithful into the compelling love of Christ and sets them on fire' (par. 10). This divine energy is directed towards promoting the work of the Church which Christ associates with himself in his work of redemption of men and glorification of the Father (cf. parr. 5, 7, 10). The Constitution therefore continues: 'From the liturgy therefore, and especially from the Eucharist, as from a fount, grace is poured forth upon us; and the sanctification of men in Christ and the glorification of God to which all other activities of the Church are directed as towards their end, are achieved in the most efficacious way possible.' (par. 10).

The author of this paper wishes to acknowledge his indebtedness to the following works:

J. Alfrink, 'The Biblical Background to the Eucharist as a Sacrificial Meal,' *Irish Theological Quarterly*, 26 (1959), 290–302.

K. Baltzer, *Das Bundesformular*, Neukirchen 1960.

R. de Vaux, *Ancient Israel*, London 1961.

W. Eichrodt, *Theology of the Old Testament*, 1, (E. tr.), London 1961.

Annie Jaubert, *La notion d'Alliance dans le judaisme aux abords de l'ère chrétienne*, Paris 1963.

J. Jeremias, *The Eucharistic Words of Jesus*, Oxford 1955.

J. L'Hour, 'L'Alliance de Sichem,' *Revue Biblique*, 69 (1962), 5–36; 161–84; 350–68.

D. J. McCarthy, S.J., *Treaty and Covenant*, Rome 1963.

'Three Covenants in Genesis,' *Catholic Biblical Quarterly*, 26 (1964), 179–89.

J. Lécuyer, *Le Sacrifice de la Nouvelle Alliance*, Paris 1962.

Various articles in Kittel's *Theologisches Wörterbuch zum Neuen Testament*.

THE PRIMACY OF CHARITY

Enda McDonagh

That charity enjoys a certain primacy in God's revelation of himself in the Old and New Testaments scarcely requires any demonstration for Christians. The two great commandments, as Christ calls them,[1] and which sum up for him the whole law and the prophets, were explicitly taken from the law, the law of the Old Testament or Mosaic Covenant.[2] In Christ's teaching they were expressly joined together, given a new extension and depth, but they had their place in the life of the old Israel as in that of the new. And the motif which dominates the relationship between God and the first people of his choice, is that of love, the love of a faithful husband for a frequently faithless wife.[3]

This faithful love achieved the climax of its expression when the Father sent his only-begotten Son.[4] And the understanding of this love and the range of its application underwent such a development that Christ could speak of it as his new commandment [5] and the distinguishing feature of his followers for the whole world.[6] In his person, life and teaching, Christ reveals the scope and demands of charity in the life and behaviour of his followers. And the theological reflection recorded in John's

[1] *Matt.* 22: 34–40; *Mark* 12: 28–34; *Luke* 10: 25–28.

[2] *Deut.* 6: 5; *Lev.* 19: 18.

[3] Cf. *Hos.* 1–3.

[4] *John* 3: 16.

[5] *John* 18: 34.

[6] *John* 13: 35.

First Epistle underlines the implications of the new commandment as he insists on love of the neighbour as the ultimate criterion of love of God.[7] For Paul the more excellent way of charity gives meaning to everything else that a man does.[8] It is the bond of perfection [9] in which all the other moral precepts are fulfilled.[10]

In attempting a scientific account of the behaviour demanded of Christ's followers, moral theology must in its general and special sections accord to charity the recognition given to it by Christ and the inspired writers. To explore what this recognition means and why it may be described as the primacy of charity in moral theology, is the purpose of this paper. The pursuit of this purpose must be within the general framework of the God-Christ-man relationship and of the invitation-response structure which underlies the Christian life and moral theology.

A DIVINE GIFT

There is of course nothing that we have not received from God.[11] The whole of creation is a reflection of God, some communication, however inadequate, of the divine goodness. Man created in the image of God,[12] enjoying at the human-created level capacities to know and love, so characteristic of God himself, must be regarded as the omega-point of God's gift of creation. Yet to talk of charity or Christian love as a divine gift is to transcend the created and human for the divine itself, to move from reflection and image to that which is reflected and imaged. Charity is God abroad in the world.[13] It is a divine gift, a gift by the divine of the divine.

The two primary commandments for man are his love of God

[7] 1 *John* 3: 17; 4: 20–21.
[8] 1 *Cor.* 12: 31; 13: 1 ff.
[9] *Col.* 3: 14.
[10] *Rom.* 13: 8–10; *Gal.* 5: 14.
[11] 1 *Cor.* 4: 7.
[12] *Gen.* 1: 26.
[13] 1 *John* 4: 16.

and his love of the neighbour for God's sake. But they are secondary to and derivative from God's love of him. The agape-love of the New Testament to which man is summoned springs from God's love of man. ' In this is love, not that we loved God, but that he loved us.' [14] God's approach to man in love in the Old and New Testaments, which is recounted in the history of salvation, has a transforming effect on man. This presence of God to man in love enables man to love in return. ' See what love the Father has given us that we should be called the children of God, as so we are.' [15]

Love awakens love. The love of the Father for man awakens in him a new capacity to love. Man receives not only a new grasp of God's lovableness, so that he may be stimulated to a greater intensity of love. He is caught up by the power of God's love into loving as God does. God's communication of love is a communication of the power to love as Christ loves, as God loves.[16] So man becomes in a superhuman way like to God, sharing the divine love, participating in the internal divine life. In his offer of love God offers and communicates himself, for God is love. In responding to this communication man loves with the love of God. The charity which unites him to God and his fellowman comes entirely from God. For it is ' God's love (which) has been poured forth into our hearts through the Holy Spirit which has been given to us.' [17]

THE PERSONAL QUALITY OF CHARITY

The divine gift which is charity presupposes a certain capacity in man. It is only because man is a loving creature that he can be admitted to sharing the love of the creator. The spiritual dimension which distinguishes man from the most highly developed animal or the most intricate machine and which

[14] 1 *John* 4: 10.
[15] 1 *John* 3: 1; cf. *Rom.* 8: 16; *John* 3: 10.
[16] Cf. *John* 15: 9–12.
[17] *Rom.* 5: 5.

constitutes him a person, enables him to love. Love is a relationship between persons. It is in fact *the* relationship between them. Only persons can love and be loved.

A love relationship is easier to recognize in the concrete than to analyse in the abstract. Witnessing the love of a mother for her child, of friend for friend, of husband for wife can be far more enlightening than any abstract discussion. Yet to understand the gift of charity, it is necessary to examine more fully the nature and characteristics of love at this human and personal level.

Love may be generally described as a profound personal recognition of and inclination towards another person seeking unity with him. This movement arises from the depth of one's personality where mind and will and feeling merge. Love offers self to the other in search of unity. Where the love is mutual, unity is achieved; a community is formed.

The personal reaction of love for another begins with some recognition, however implicit and inarticulate, of the loved one as valuable in himself, an end in himself and not just a means. This value derives from his unique, irreplaceable character and the autonomy which he enjoys as a spiritual being.

Part of creation and so reflecting the divine, part of the human race and so an image of God, each human being enjoys personal uniqueness before God and so before other men. He reflects and images God in a way impossible to anything or anybody else. He is the incarnation of a human spirit with an unrepeated name and destiny, an irreproducible capacity to love. Genuine love requires this uniqueness. It does not love mankind. It loves men, particular people, whom it recognizes in this personal way. A mother loves her children not in general but each of them in a special, individual way.

Closely related to this unique quality of the person is his autonomy. Through his spiritual endowment he possesses the power of self-determination, the right to dispose of self, to commit himself. He and no other human being is master of his destiny. This is the meaning of his freewill. (In both his uniqueness and his autonomy, he is manifesting in the highest earthly form the one, omnipotent God.) The personal reaction of love recognizes this autonomy. It never seeks to possess or use a person as one might possess or use a thing. The possessive mother or lover is so far deficient in love. The loved one may not be sought for self-satisfaction, used just to fulfil one's needs. Such a movement would imprison the beloved (and indeed the lover) and destroy his autonomy. His integrity as a person is violated. Instead of being accepted as a person (a thou or you, in the Buber terminology), he becomes a thing (an it).[18]

The opening out to or movement towards the other in this way which is the beginning of love, demands further expression in care and service.[19] The care and service take different forms in different relationships. Not all loving care can be manifested in the same tender way as a mother's care for her new-born child. Not all mothers with a genuine love of their children will have the same manner or degree of tender care. But without care and service, love remains notional and unreal, a love of self perhaps or a love of the idea of love. The service also implies taking some responsibility for the beloved. His good becomes the personal concern of the lover, who will make his own the task of fostering that good and removing the dangers that threaten it.

Love draws the person out of himself towards the other in recognizing and caring for the other and seeking unity with him. This movement outwards enables the person who loves to grow and develop. Without it he remains confined within himself, unable to expand as a person. In this sense a person needs to love. And since love is something which is gradually developed, and since it is essentially a response to another person, it flourishes only where there is a return of love. A person also needs to be loved. It is through loving that the person expresses himself most fully, that he attains his highest fulfilment as a person. It is by being loved that his own love and capacity to love are completed

[18] Cf. M. Buber, *I and Thou*, Edinburgh, 1937.
[19] Cf. E. Fromm, *The Art of Loving*, London, 1962, 25–6.

and reassured. Love is the necessary perfection of the person and it is love which stimulates or creates love.

Here some brief reference to the age-old discussion on the distinction between the giving and the receiving aspects of love is necessary. Does somebody love for what he gets or for what he gives? Is love a form of desire, a search for something for oneself, some pleasure or satisfaction, or is it disinterested giving to another? The discussion has been carried on in the context of merely human love and of Christian charity. St Thomas [20] distinguished between a love of desire, *amor concupiscentiae*, which sought primarily the good of the lover, and love of benevolence, *amor benevolentiae*, which sought primarily the good of the beloved. The distinction was described by C. S. Lewis [21] as that of 'need love' and 'gift love' and a similar distinction is basic to Nygren's important work, *Agape and Eros*.[22]

Because man needs to love and to be loved, it might seem that his love is necessarily a 'need love' or selfish love. But this is to misunderstand the personality of man and his need to love. In his human endowment man has been given the capacity to recognize and love the other for the other's sake, as a unique autonomous person, valuable in himself. In doing this the lover is both giving and receiving. But he receives only to the extent that he gives. The disinterested self-giving is primary, but can be achieved in varying degrees and only gradually. If however he simply seeks his own satisfaction, he does not love in authentic fashion and he fails to break out of his self-enclosure and reach the other as another person.[23] He remains confined within this self-centred circle and is unable to expand and develop. His attempt to love only for his own sake destroys love and prevents his normal personal fulfilment.

The divine love which man shares in charity, respects his human condition and operates through it. But a new superhuman

[20] Cf. *S. theol.* I, II, q. 26, a. 4 etc.

[21] C. S. Lewis, *The Four Loves*, London, 1960.

[22] London, 1951.

[23] Amans fit extra se in amatum translatus.

dimension has been introduced. In the loving relationship with the personal God which he enjoys, the recognition and service and self-giving are not from his own resources. He has been admitted to the personal life and love of the Trinity, so that he loves in some measure as God loves. His love of human persons has been transformed in this way also, so that he sees and loves them as God sees and loves them. His recognition and service and love still depend on his human faculties and human activities; but they have been deepened by faith, so that he recognizes more deeply the value and lovableness (the divine lovableness) of each person, and seeks unity with them under the impelling force of God's love for them.

At this divine level also the apparent conflict between 'need love' and 'gift love' is more clearly transcended.[24] The total giving of the divine persons to each other without losing their identity as persons provides the supreme model of 'gift love.' It is on this model and through enjoying some share in the actual trinitarian love and giving, that man gives himself in charity to God and his fellowmen.

CHRISTIAN LOVE

Charity is God's love abroad in the world. It is the presence of God in love to the human person, asking for love in response. It is the presence of God in love within the human person, seeking expression through his human and personal activity. It was in Christ that this loving presence of God to man and man's loving response achieved supreme realization. It is by each man's union with Christ that the divine love enters his heart and elicits his response. Christ is the love-link between God and man; God's communication of himself as love to man. In the person and life of Christ charity entered fully into man's world.

It was out of love for the world, for man, in the desire to share his divine, eternal life with him, that God sent his only

[24] V. Warnach: *Agape: Liebe als Grundmotiv der neutestamentlichen Theologie*, Düsseldorf, 1951, 462 ff.

Son.[25] This initiative born of love was all the more striking in that it was while we were yet sinners,[26] that ' God sent his only Son into the world so that we might live through him.' [27] The plan of salvation for man which the Father accomplished in Christ, was at once a manifestation of the divine love and an invitation to love. It manifested the divine love by manifesting the God who is love. Christ reveals the Father. He who sees him, sees the Father.[28] He who hates him, hates the Father.[29] No one can come in love to the Father except through him.[30] If a man loves him, Christ and the Father will love him and they will come and dwell with him.[31] He himself manifested the highest love for the Father [32] and for man by laying down his life for man [33] to atone for man's previous rejection of God and restore him to the Father. And in his return to the Father he sent as he had promised the Spirit,[34] the mutual love-gift of Father and Son. The reception of this Spirit, variously called the ' Spirit of God,'[35] the ' Spirit of Christ,' [36] ' Spirit of the Son,' [37] completed the admission of his friends to the divine life, giving them the rank of sons of the Father and brothers of Christ.[38]

In his personal life and teaching Christ gave his followers the example and instruction by which they were to fulfil the two great commandments. Through his death and resurrection he assured them of the power to follow this example and instruction.

[25] *John* 3: 16.
[26] *Rom.* 5: 8; cf. *Eph.* 2: 4–5.
[27] 1 *John* 4: 9.
[28] *John* 14: 9.
[29] *John* 15: 23.
[30] *John* 14: 6.
[31] *John* 14: 23.
[32] *John* 14: 31.
[33] *John* 15: 13.
[34] *John* 14: 16.
[35] *Rom.* 8: 9, 14; *Eph.* 4: 30.
[36] *Rom.* 8: 9.
[37] *Gal.* 4: 6.
[38] *Rom.* 8: 15; *Eph.* 4: 6–7.

By abiding in the vine and sharing its life Christians bear fruit [39] in the recognition and service and union of love with God and man. By being united with their head in one body [40] they experience the impulse of the love that was in Christ. In this way they are able to fulfil his new commandment [41] to love as he loves, as sons of the Father and brothers of Christ.

The divine love was always active in the world, even after man's sin. The whole history of salvation testifies to the persistence of the Father in seeking man's love. The promise of a redeemer after man's initial failure, the slow patient fulfilment of that promise in the call of Abraham, the definitive call of the people of Israel in the Exodus and in the giving of the Mosaic law, the sending of the prophets—these provided continual reminders and manifestations of God's love. In his instructions and commandments also the God of Israel, the God of the Old Testament, revealed the importance of love. Yet it was with the sending of his Son that his love and he himself as love were fully manifested to man and the power to share that love made freely available to him.

A CRUCIFIED LOVE

Christian love is born in the shadow of the cross, where Christ for love of man finally and totally surrendered himself in love to the Father. It was for this that he came into the world, to do the will of him who sent him 'so that the world might know that (he) loves the Father.' [42] The fulfilment of the Father's will to save mankind involved placing a certain distance between himself and the Father. He came out from the Father to share man's lowly and unglorified condition. Although he was the only-begotten Son he emptied himself, taking the form of a servant, like to man in all things except sin.[43] He was to return to the

[39] *John* 15: 1 ff.
[40] 1 *Cor.* 12: 12–27; *Eph.* 4: 1–16.
[41] *John* 13: 34.
[42] *John* 14: 31.
[43] *Phil.* 2: 6–7.

Father and share again the glory which was his from the beginning.[44] But his very return was the way of fallen mankind, the way of disintegration and death. In accepting humanity he also accepted death. The particularly painful and brutal death which Christ experienced impresses on us the extent of his love. But the primary fact is that he died. God-made-man died. He went to his Father through the way imposed on man for his sin,[45] and he experienced all the fear and agony which are man's facing the wrenching apart of body and spirit. He shrank from it, as men do. He begged the Father to save him from it, if possible.[46] He cried out in abandonment during the last moments.[47] Christ was not playing at being a man. He was fully human and paid the price of his humanity in leaving this world.

Some other way of reconciling man with God could have been devised. But the effectiveness of the way chosen may at least be partially grasped. In the undeniable reality of Christ's human life taken to its bitter end, in the personal acceptance of this death despite the human revulsion from it, the meaning of the divine love for mankind, of the love expected in return from man in the context of sin and its consequences, could hardly be made clearer. It is in contemplating the climax of Christ's life in his death, that one begins to appreciate 'the breadth and length and height and depth' of his love, a love 'that surpasses knowledge,' and by which 'we are filled with the fullness of God.'[48]

It was necessary in the Father's plan for Christ to pass through the separation of death to enter into the glory of the Resurrection.[49] The reconciliation and reunion of God and man at Christ's glorification in the Resurrection were achieved for sinful mankind through Christ's sacrifice of himself on the cross.[50] Whoever would follow Christ[51] in his loving surrender to the Father,

[44] *John* 17: 5, 24.
[45] *Rom.* 5: 12.
[46] *Matt.* 26: 39.
[47] *Matt.* 27: 46.
[48] *Eph.* 3: 18–19.
[49] *Luke* 24: 26.
[50] *Rom.* 5: 10–11; *Eph.* 2: 13–16.
[51] *Matt.* 16: 24 par.

must understand that the way of Christian love, as marked out by Christ, is the way of the cross.

Christians are baptized into the passion, death and resurrection of Christ.[52] Their Christian life is a living out of these redemptive mysteries in their own life. Their identification with Christ in his total giving of himself to the Father is realized first of all in the sacramental meeting with Christ. Each sacrament provides its particular contact with Christ in the mystery of his self-giving and the Father's acceptance through death and resurrection. The basic sacramental introduction to Christ in his redemptive activity takes place at baptism, gateway to the Church and to the other sacraments. Its climax is reached in the Eucharist which makes present not merely Christ in action, acting on the recipient, but Christ in person, and unites man directly to the redemptive sacrifice of the cross and its glorious completion.

Christian love then is stamped with the sign of the cross. The sacramental way of union with Christ emphasizes this. But behind the cross lies man's sin. In the divine plan, Christ's death was the result of man's sin.[53] Man by his rejection of God had lost contact with the focal point of his existence and of his love. His capacity and need to love were frustrated. His love, cut off from its ultimate, meaningful term in the person of God, turned in on himself. He became imprsioned in the self, unable of himself to reach even other human persons in complete love-relationships. It was in this failure to love others with the disinterested recognition and service which such love implies, that man's sin made itself most evident in his human activity. His essential humanity remained, but because his personal link with God had been broken, his other personal links lacked vitality. To break out of the circle of self became increasingly difficult, and other people tended to become objects of satisfaction, things to be used rather than persons to be loved.

The break-through from self to the Father and to other men

[52] *Rom.* 6: 3 ff.

[53] *Rom.* 5: 6 ff., etc.

was achieved supremely for sinful man by Christ. In the climax of his self-giving, in his passion and death, Christ taught man how he must die to self to reach the other and so love in a fully personal way. Breaking out of the shell of selfishness in which he has become fixed through sin and its consequences, is a very painful process for man. The pain is completed by death to the old self-centred sinful man,[54] who is crucified.[55] Thereby man rises with Christ to a new life.[56] He is a new man,[57] a new creation.[58] The share in Christ's death and resurrection which is man's through the sacraments must be translated into his every-day activity. The pain and death will be no longer simply his in sign and in the presence of Christ with him, but in the experience of trying to give himself after the manner of Christ to God and his neighbour. Every attempt to do this will involve suffering, the suffering of placing others before oneself, of letting go of oneself to reach the others. Gradually man through the power of Christ's love will acquire mastery over himself. He will become in spirit and action another son of God, liberated from the slavery of sin and of self. But the process will be slow and painful, making continuous demands upon him in his every human act and contact. Each day he has to die to self overcoming his selfish tendencies, giving himself out of love to the recognition and service of God and mankind. But it is by dying with Christ in this way that he experiences the joy of Christ's resurrection, losing his life to find it anew in the joy [59] and peace [60] and liberty [61] of the sons of God.

[54] *Rom.* 6: 5–6.
[55] *Gal.* 5: 24.
[56] *Rom.* 6: 4; *Col.* 21: 12 ff., etc.
[57] *Eph.* 2: 15.
[58] 2 *Cor.* 5: 17. For this relationship between Christian love and death and resurrection cf. Warnach, *op. cit.* 371 ff.
[59] *John* 16: 20–24; *Rom.* 14: 17; 15: 13.
[60] *John* 14: 27; *Rom.* 14: 17; 15: 13.
[61] *Rom.* 8: 21; 2 *Cor.* 3: 17.

LOVE OF GOD AND OF MAN

The object of charity, its personal term, is both God and man. This was already laid down in the Mosaic law, although the immediate linking of the two commandments and their recognition as summarizing the whole law was only made explicit in the new law. The further implications of the New Testament relation between those commandments gradually emerge in the teaching of Jesus and his apostles.

Love of man, of the neighbour, assumes a new significance as the test of one's love of God. No man can claim to love God unless he has a genuine love of his neighbour.[62] Jesus' description of his second coming and man's final judgment [63] makes this very clear. Our living recognition and service of Christ depends on recognition and service of him in the poor and needy who inhabit our world. To fail these people is to fail Christ. To ignore their poverty, illness, and other needs is to ignore Christ.

The image of God in the neighbour, source of his personality, his uniqueness and his lovableness, has received a new depth through the incarnation. All men are now called to be sons of the Father. They must be loved and served as Christ must be loved and served, as they share his sonship and lovableness. This applies to all mankind. There can be no distinction of race or class or creed. One must love all as Christ loves them, even one's enemies,[64] so that the Christian return for hate, persecution and death is love. 'Father forgive them . . .'[65]

The love of neighbour required of Christians is clearly an active love. The emphasis in Jesus' account of the final judgment, as in his parable of the good Samaritan,[66] is on the need to express love in service of the poor and needy. The sins of omission loom much larger here than they are allowed to in the conventional Christian exhortation. To ignore and neglect the hungry, the

[62] 1 *John* 4: 20.
[63] *Matt.* 25: 31–46.
[64] *Matt.* 5: 43–48.
[65] *Luke* 23: 34.
[66] *Luke* 10: 29–37.

sick, the homeless, the under-privileged of any kind, merits Christ's 'Depart from me.' *Matthew* 25 should make disturbing reading for the comfortable Western Christian, lay or cleric, who preserves his peace of mind by playing down the victimization that is all about him, or who invokes a misguided prudence in support of the status quo and inactivity, even if it is called 'gradualness.' The vitality of Christianity (for example, of Christian love) in any society and in the whole world is measured not by external religious trappings, but by the dynamic efforts of the strong (strong politically, financially or educationally) to help, in the name of Christ, the weak.

Christian love demands service but it must be personal service, as the love is personal. Charity does not mean primarily dispensing alms or providing social service. It is first of all recognizing, respecting and committing oneself to a person. It may happen in a fleeting encounter, yet the respect and reverence and love for the other will be sufficient to manifest the community which exists between all men in Christ. Just as it is possible to degrade a person by using him as an object or possession, so it is possible to give help in an impersonal and degrading way. Without genuine concern and love for the person in need, the assistance becomes a form of self-satisfaction for the individual or society. Love and service go together. And true love demands efficient service, the organized assistance of the weak in today's complex world. But such assistance must always recognize the first need of these people, to be treated and respected and loved as people.

Love is a relation between persons. It involves the whole person, his mind in recognizing the person, his will in self-commitment to him, his emotions in support of both. Where mind and will and feeling harmonize, love flourishes. But if the recognition of the other as a person, and as this particular person, is weak or undeveloped, or if the will to commitment is hampered by self-will, or if there is some emotional reaction against the other, love is weak and may perish.

The pulpit cliché, 'You must love but need not like,' can be very misleading here. The accompanying explanation that love is an act of the will not of the emotions, and that you cannot control or at least command your likes and dislikes, is inadequate. The act of choice by the will is the finally decisive element in love. And one can love even where there is emotional revulsion. But this is an abnormal situation. Love is an activity of the whole person and the will is heavily conditioned by mental and emotional reaction of the person. Unless an attempt is made to resolve the emotional dislike, the love will not survive for long, as the person's thought, speech and activity may quickly demonstrate. Christian living should normally involve liking, or at least gradually remove any disliking of persons.[67]

CHARITY AND THE OTHER VIRTUES

The supremacy of charity in the Christian life and amongst the virtues is incontestable as far as the evidence of revelation goes. In the theological understanding of this, there have been various stages of development. A climax was reached in medieval theology with St Thomas. His description [68] of charity as mother, basis and root of all the virtues received its full doctrinal expression in his teaching on charity as the form of the virtues.[69] Today, after many changes of direction and some very mistaken attempts to give charity its due place, a fresh attempt is being made to probe the relationship between charity and the other virtues in the Christian ethic.

The primacy of Christian charity over the other virtues derives from the place of love as man's supreme personal activity, and the essentially divine character of Christian love as a share in the divine love. Through it man loves with the love of God himself. But this love must be active, express itself in reverence and

[67] As Spicq points out (*Agape in the New Testament*, I London, 1963, 11) one must distinguish *agapan* and *philein*, which as the love of friendship implies some affection and warmth of feeling. Yet the full human realization of agape is incompatible with emotional dislike or resentment.

[68] Cf. *S. theol.* I, II, q. 62; II, II, q. 23.

[69] *S. theol.* II, II, q. 23, a. 8c.

service of God and man. The explicit teaching of the New Testament as well as the peculiar nature of man as a material-spiritual being who expresses himself and develops through his human activity, make it clear that charity requires the various activities of the other virtues of justice, truth, chastity and the rest. That charity must be active is, as was pointed out above,[70] a basic Christian requirement. So any form of quietism, which would suppress all other human activity in favour of pure acts of charity, cannot be reconciled with Christ's own teaching and has been very properly condemned by the Church.[71]

A different and more subtle misunderstanding of the primacy of charity has been given new vitality in recent times. It accepts the other virtues of justice, chastity etc., and some formulations of their content and limits in commands and prohibitions, as general guide-lines for the Christian man. But these formulations of limits in the prohibition of fornication, for example, can never be absolute. What is ultimately decisive in an ethical situation, is how far the activity contemplated is an expression of love. And one can never a *priori* rule out any particular activity such as fornication, as always and ever incompatible with true Christian love and, therefore, as absolutely forbidden. In ninety-nine cases out of a hundred perhaps it will be so, but there is the possibility of the hundredth case.[72]

This approach, a form of 'situation ethics' rife in Europe in the forties and fifties, has come very much to the fore amongst English-speaking Christians just now, through the writings of the Bishop of Woolwich,[73] Canon Douglas Rhymes [74] and others. There should be no denying the merit of their approach in emphasizing again the central rôle of charity for too long neglected in the conventional Catholic moral teaching at least. The

[70] V. supra, p. 142f.

[71] *Denz. Schön.* 2181 ff.; 2201 ff.

[72] Cf. J. A. T. Robinson, *Honest to God*, London, 1963, 118; D. A. Williams. 'Theology and Self-Awareness' in A. Vidler, (Ed.) *Soundings*, Cambridge, 1962, 81.

[73] Robinson, *op. cit.*, *id. Christian Morals Today*, London, 1964.

[74] *No New Morality*, London, 1964.

preoccupation for so long with the physical integrity of sexual acts, for example, together with the neglect of the more fundamental problem of whether this act was a genuine expression of Christian love, provides a classic instance of the type of Christian moral teaching against which the bishop and the canon were reacting. Yet their ethic, despite its apparent support from Augustine's summary of Christian living, *ama et fac quod vis*, empties love of any real meaning, ignores man's human condition and is ultimately opposed to the teaching of the New Testament.

To maintain that while love generally expresses itself in a particular way and generally excludes certain actions, but that there are no actions which could not in certain circumstances be compatible with it, does seem as Herbert McCabe points out, to make love meaningless.[75] If, for example, ' rape ' or ' cruelty to children,' carefully defined of course, could be regarded as expressions of love in some conceivable circumstances, love loses all meaning. If they could not, then there are some absolutes in the Christian ethic, some activities absolutely forbidden, some limits to the behaviour which can be an expression of love. Genuine Christian love then demands avoidance of such behaviour. Virtues and vices, commands and prohibitions, retain their reality under the primacy of love.

The deeper basis for this lies in man's human condition. Created in God's image with a capacity to know, to commit himself freely, to love, called to a divine destiny to share in the divine knowledge and love, man is a complex material-spiritual creature. He is a social being, destined to enter the world and develop in it through relationships with others. He is a sexual being. He is a being in time, who develops gradually. Within this divinely-given structure man seeks his destiny, seeks to express, through the human faculties or powers with which he has been endowed, the divine love given to him. The expression of this love from God is possible only through the human faculties also received from God. So it is possible to see that not every

[75] H. McCabe, 'The Cartesian Basis of the New Morality,' *Blackfriars*, May 1964, 194 ff.

conceivable act respects this divinely-given structure and so some such actions could not be ways of communicating charity. What precisely these forbidden actions are or how far they extend may be difficult to determine, although there is a long history of human reflection on this problem with some fairly widespread agreement on matters like murder, lying, adultery.

However it is in the New Testament that any doubts about whether love suppresses in this 'situation' sense the need for the other virtues, are removed. Jesus is very insistent that whoever loves must keep his commandments,[76] and these are often a reaffirmation, extension and deepening of the commandments received by Moses from Jahweh.[77] They clearly include the prohibition of those actions which could not possibly be bearers or expressions of Christian love because they defile man,[78] and which are listed by St Paul as evil and excluding from the kingdom of heaven.[79] The explicit teaching of the New Testament and its authentication for succeeding generations by Christ's Church, demonstrate the possible and impossible ways of communicating Christian charity. In their positive content and negative limits, the other virtues have an irreplaceable rôle in Christian life as a life of love.

The primary rôle of love in the Christian life as giving all other virtues their true Christian or divine significance [80] has been expressed in St Thomas's doctrine of charity as the *forma omnium virtutum*. The moral goodness of a particular human activity or virtue is derived from its relation to man's last end.[81] It is this relation which basically gives the act or virtue its form.[82]

[76] *John* 14: 15.

[77] Cf. *Matt.* 5: 17–48.

[78] *Mark* 7: 20–23. And he said 'What comes out of a man is what defiles a man. For from within, out of the heart of man come evil thoughts, fornication, theft, murder, adultery, coveting, wickedness, deceit, licentiousness, envy, slander, pride, foolishness. All these evil things come from within and they defile a man.'

[79] *Rom.* 1: 28–31; *Gal.* 5: 19–21.

[80] Cf. 1 *Cor.* 13: *S. theol.* II, II, q. 23, a. 7, c. Nulla vera virtus potest esse sine caritate.

[81] II II, q. 23, a. 7, c.

[82] II II, q. 23, a. 8, c.

But this relation is the relation of charity uniting the human agent with God as his last end. So charity constitutes the 'form' of all the virtues, as well as being the mother which nourishes them, the foundation on which they are laid, the root from which they grow.[83]

One understanding of St Thomas's teaching regards this relation to the last end given to a virtuous act by charity as extrinsic to the act itself. A man performs these acts out of charity, for love of God. Acts of justice and of the other virtues are referred to God from the outside by the human agent. Charity does not enter into the object of the act in an intrinsic way.

The recent work of Gerard Gillemann [84] has challenged this both as an adequate explanation of the relationship between charity and the other virtues and as a correct understanding of St Thomas. For him the relationship is intrinsic, in the very act itself, so that this action of justice, for example, is a mediation of charity in this sphere of life. The acts of the other virtues are mediations or communications of charity in different areas of life. In this line of argument the object of any particular virtue is a particular *finis*, *bonum* or value which derives its meaning and existence from the supreme value, the *summum bonum* or *finis ultimus* God. The fundamental relationship of the person to God which is charity, is mediated or participated in by the particular virtue or activity which relates the person to this particular good of, for example, justice or chastity.

In revealing the internal dynamism of charity as it seeks expression through man's human endowment in the various virtuous activities, Gillemann has done a great service to moral theology. And he has shown fairly convincingly that the divine love is not merely a source of inspiration or motivation, but the very motor-force [85] or efficient cause [86] which finds expression in all the Christian's good acts; so that these acts are in the

[83] *Ibid.*
[84] *The Primacy of Charity in Moral Theology*, London, 1959.
[85] Cf. *De Virt* 2, 3c. Caritas est motor omnium virtutum.
[86] Gillemann, *op. cit.*, 35.

abstract to be regarded as good if they are capable of being expressions of the divine love in man. Man's complex make-up, and the complexity of particular goods or values through which he is perfected, demand different forms of such expression, just as they rule out others.

Difficulties about the distinction of the other virtues from charity, and the meaning of 'virtuous' activity in somebody without charity, are not insuperable. To the plurality of particular values or ends open to man in his complexity, must be added his temporal character, his living in time. It is only gradually, one step after another, that man, entering into himself, taking possession of himself, achieves these particular values. He can achieve any or all of these in some degree without attaining the supreme virtue of his being, his giving of himself as a whole in love. But the realization of these particular values by acts of justice or truth or chastity are directed towards and need to be completed in love. It is as expressions of love that they are fully acts of any particular virtue. These points are further developed in a recent article by Karl Rahner,[87] who goes on to stress an important distinction between charity and the other virtues.[88] While the other virtues demand certain actions from a man, charity demands himself. The other virtues gradually grow through exercise, but may be satisfied here and now by a particular action. Charity must be always growing and can never rest satisfied with the status quo. He who decides that he has given all in love, and that he cannot and will not love any more, has not really given all and does not love, as Christ commands, 'with all his heart and all his soul, with all his mind and all his strength.'[89]

[87] 'Das "Gebot" der Liebe unter der anderen Geboten,' *Schriften zur Theologie*, V. Zurich-Köln, 1962, 494–517.

[88] *Loc. cit.*, 507 ff.

[89] *Mark* 12–31; cf. *Matt.* 22: 37; *Luke* 10: 27.

CONCLUSION

To recognize the primacy of charity in the Christian life and in moral theology is to follow the spirit and the letter of the New Testament. The fuller understanding of charity as the Father's gift of the divine love, given to each man in Christ by the sending of the Spirit, and involving man in the pain and joy of Christ's death and resurrection, reveals the Christian's source of life and strength. It indicates what is precisely divine and Christian about him, his admission to the divine family as a son of the Father and brother of Christ. This divine and Christian element in him seeks expression through all his human powers and activities. It gives them their eternal relevance, as elements in the process of his christification, his gradual attainment of the fullness of life which the Son shares with the Father and the Holy Spirit.

The Father has invited all men to share this life in his Son. The mission of the Son, sent out of love, dedicating himself in love to the service of mankind, finally sacrificing himself in love to the Father for man—this mission continues to the end. But the Son is no longer physically present, no longer visible to the man whom he would have to share his life. It is in the members of his body, united with him and with each other that the sacrificial love of Christ for mankind is now made visible. This is the sign of his disciples. It is this love, Christ's own love in his members, that must mediate the divine presence to men and evoke their love in return. The mission of the Church, of Christians is to awaken men to the sense of God's presence among them by the force of Christian charity. For charity is God's presence in the world. Therein lies its primacy.

THE MEANING OF JUSTICE

Denis O'Callaghan

This paper proposes to analyse the concept of justice and to discover the place of justice in the Christian life. I feel that an undertaking of this kind has a special relevance for the modern theologian. The need for renewal in moral theology is widely felt, the renewal process has already begun, but as yet there is no marked hardening of doctrine in the various departments. The new approaches have introduced a new atmosphere, a new sense into our theology, but the implications have not been worked out in the many provinces of Christian living. While the pre-eminence of charity has been high-lighted, the rôle of the other virtues in mediating charity is still quite obscure. Is there some risk that these virtues will lose their identity and definition in the final synthesis?

In the idealist, perfectionist outlook of the theology of charity, the rigid, legalistic virtue of justice can be embarrassing to a degree. Here is a virtue of limits, of minima, of inflexible lines marking off mine and thine. Can it preserve its validity in the new scheme of things? Marc Tremeau in his *Principes de morale chrétienne* gives just one sentence to justice. Many of the modern authors who treat the question at greater length do not appear quite at ease. One senses a certain note of apology if they have to introduce perfectly valid but 'abstract' philosophical or theological distinctions. They may employ new terms; but is there a note of camouflage here? Nothing is to be gained by swinging the pendulum from one extreme to the other. If our moral theology is to be scientific and realistic it must make use of all the resources of the divine word and of human reason. Understanding can be achieved by an analysis not only of what God has revealed in Christ, but by what he has revealed to us in the intelligence of an Aristotle or of a St Thomas.

THE ANSWER OF HISTORY

The Graeco-Roman philosophers saw in justice the primary value of human action and the very measure of civilization. Justice is the principle which orders man's relations to his fellows and which inspires the laws that guarantee the equilibrium and tranquillity of the community. In a word, the just is equivalent to the good. Aristotle quotes the proverb: 'Justice sums up all virtues in itself,' and he honours it with the tribute that neither Hesperus (the evening star) nor Lucifer (the morning star) is quite as beautiful as this queen of the virtues.[1] In Cicero's *De Officiis* we find a similar appreciation: 'In justitia virtutis splendor est maximus, ex qua boni viri nominantur; haec enim una virtus omnium est domina et regina virtutum.'[2]

When the Greek philosophers attributed this absolute primacy to justice they were employing the term in its more general sense as a principle of harmony in the community. Plato's just man is he who performs the task or function proper to him in accordance with his place in society.[3] For Aristotle justice connotes conformity with law because this produces and preserves the happiness of the community; the just man is the law-abiding man.[4]

[1] *Nicomachaean Ethics* 5, 1, 15 (Trans. by F. H. Peters, London, 1891). The quotation 'Εν δὲ δικαιοσύνῃ συλλήβδην πᾶσ' ἀρετή is from the sixth-century poet Theognis.

[2] *De Officiis* 1: 7; 3: 6.

[3] *Republic* 4, 10, 433A τό τὰ αὐτοῦ πράττειν.

[4] 'The laws prescribe about all manner of things aiming at the common interest of all . . . and so in one sense we apply the term *just* to whatever tends to produce and preserve the happiness of the community' (*Nic. Eth.* 5, 1, 13).

Del Vecchio, a great authority on law and justice, offers the following explanation:

> The rapid and unanimous recognition of justice as universal virtue is explained by the latitude which belongs to the concept, which understood as a mere principle of order and harmony, is not concerned with any particular motive, and does not prescribe any definite attitude or mode of behaviour, but expresses only the requirement that *that shall happen which ought (ethically) to happen*, that there be an exact correspondence between the fact and the norm which applies to it. [5]

In the Judaeo-Christian tradition we encounter an even wider concept of justice. Firstly, there is the justice of God. In the order of eternity this denotes the intrinsic harmony of the divine will, the fact that God acts according to the norms and directions of his nature. In the order of time it means that he is faithful to the promises made in his covenants with man, that he will reward the good and punish the evildoer :

> ' God is faithful and without any iniquity, he is just and right.' [6]
> ' I am the Lord who exercise mercy and judgment and justice on the earth.' [7]

Corresponding to this justice of God there is a justice of man. In both the Old and New Testaments this justice is synonymous with virtue or perfection in general. It denotes holiness or action in conformity with the divine will, whether or not one's action has any relation to other persons.[8]

In contradistinction to this wide general concept of justice which is so conspicuous in both the Graeco-Roman and Judaeo-Christian traditions, we find a narrower and more technical concept—that of rendering to every man his due. This concept was regarded as so important for community living that justice

[5] *Justice*, Edinburgh 1952, 18.
[6] *Deut.* 32: 4.
[7] *Jer.* 9: 24.
[8] See 'Justice,' *Dictionnaire encyclopédique de la Bible*, Turnhout 1960, 1015–1020.

was numbered among the four cardinal virtues. This fourfold scheme of key virtues is encountered both in the Greek tradition of Plato and Aristotle and in the *Book of Wisdom*: 'Temperance and prudence and justice and fortitude, which are such things as man can have nothing more profitable in life.'[9] The seventh and tenth commandments of the Decalogue underline this basic obligation of respect for the right of the other, and we can see the various applications of this fundamental duty in the laws relating to justice in *Exodus* 21, 22. The Old Testament writings continually emphasize the demands which justice makes on the private individual and on the judge or superior:

'Repay thy debt and answer for it.'[10]
'Thou shalt have a just and true weight and thy bushel shall be equal and true.'[11]
'Hear them and judge that which is just whether he be one of your country or a stranger.'[12]

The New Testament repeats these precepts:

> Render therefore to all men their dues. Tribute to whom tribute is due; custom to whom custom; fear to whom fear; honour to whom honour. Owe no man anything.[13]

This same note of granting another his due is likewise central to the Graeco-Roman concept of justice in its technical sense. According to Aristotle justice enjoins an equal or fair measure:

> 'The just man is apt to aportion things, so that each shall get his fair, that is, his proportionate share.'[14]

This notion of justice as rendering to each his due is traced back at least to the sixth-century poet Simonides,[15] and it gained

[9] *Wis.* 8:7. [10] *Ecclus.* 4:8.
[11] *Deut.* 25:15.
[12] *Deut.* 1:16.
[13] *Rom.* 13:7.
[14] *Nic. Eth.* 5, 5, 18.
[15] τὸ τὰ ὀφειλόμενα ἑκάστῳ ἀποδιδόναι quoted by Plato in *Republic* 1, 6, 331E. The idea is already found in Homer, *Odyssey* 14, 84.

universal acceptance in our Western tradition through Cicero, Ambrose and Augustine.[16] The classic Scholastic definition quoted by St Thomas is a repetition of the Roman law formula: 'Justitia est constans et perpetua voluntas ius suum cuique tribuens.'[17] This tradition with its technically worked out analysis of justice was a valuable heritage for the Christian ethic, and it lent to it the support of an already accepted humanist ideal. Unfortunately it tempted the theologian to rest on his oars, and his satisfaction with what was essentially a pagan philosophy did not urge on him the necessity of working out the Christian dimensions of justice.

ANALYSIS OF JUSTICE

In the relation of justice tradition sees three essential elements: the reference to another, the satisfaction of that other's strict right, the equality produced. These elements are intimately connected, and the proper appreciation of any one of them necessarily introduces the other two. The satisfaction of a strict right is the key or central element in justice; it presupposes otherness and produces equality.

Otherness

Relation to the other is a distinctive characteristic of justice.[18] It is the function of justice to order man in his relations with his fellows. Essential to every form of justice is this inter-subjectivity, the fact that it interrelates two or more individuals by means of some external contact or transaction. Justice is always a community virtue, it is always possessed of a social, outward-looking note in that it commands one to respect the right of others and to refrain from injuring them.

[16] Cicero, *De Finibus* 5: 23; Ambrose, *De Officiis* 1: 24; Augustine, *De Civitate Dei* 19: 21.
[17] *S. theol.* II-II, 58, 1. Cf. Justinian, *Inst.* 1: 1.
[18] *Nic. Eth.* 5, 1, 3.

Right

In a relation of justice a man claims his *right* (ius, debitum); he claims something which belongs to him in such a way that everyone, whether private individual or public authority, must grant it to him and allow him to enjoy it.[19] Since it is the function of justice to respect and to grant right, right precedes and specifies justice: ' If the act of justice is to give each one his due, then the act of justice is preceded by the act whereby something becomes his due.' [20] This is self-evident. Before one party can be charged with an obligation in justice towards another, that other must have a claim or title to the given thing, a bond in virtue of which it is his own, and by which he demands it for himself. How explain this capacity by which man can claim something as exclusively his own? The explanation given by St Thomas finds the reason in the kind of creature man is: ' It is through creation that the creature first comes to have his rights.' [21] Man is the subject of rights because he is created a person by the act of God. He is a spiritual being, solitary and incommunicable, a totality in himself who is entrusted with the responsibility of his own destiny. Therefore, certain things and opportunities are due to him, and he can claim them against others as necessary means for the development of his personality and the attainment of his final end. The world, society, and civilization have no other immediate meaning than to servė man.[22] The duties of justice are a necessary consequence of man's personality and individuality. If justice is downgraded, there is an attack not just on the material order but on the very independence of man's person.

[19] 'Ratio vero justitiae consistit in hoc quod alteri reddatur quod ei debetur secundum aequalitatem' (*S. Theol.* II-II, 80, un).

[20] *S. contra Gent.*, 2, 28.

[21] *Ibid.* Cf. Cicero, *De Legibus* 5: 17 'Natura iuris . . . ab hominis repetenda est natura.'

[22] 'Sa spiritualité lui confère une dignité eminente; lui seul joue dans le monde le rôle de valeur absolue et c'est à lui qu'est subordonneé toute l'ouvre de civilisation' J.-T ‸Delos, 'Le problème des rapports du droit et de la morale,' *Arch. Phil. Dr. Soc. Jur.* 3 (1933), 98.

In *Pacem in Terris* Pope John XXIII lays down the principle:

> Every human being is a person; his nature is endowed with intelligence and free-will. By virtue of this he has rights and duties, flowing directly and simultaneously from his very nature, which are therefore universal, inviolable and inalienable.[23]

As examples of these rights he instances the right to life and to a worthy manner of living, the right to respect and education, the right to worship God according to conscience, the right to choose one's state in life, the right to private property, the right to a just wage, the right of free association, the right to emigrate, the right to take a part in public affairs. These rights occasion corresponding obligations in justice: 'To one man's right there corresponds a duty in all other persons; the duty namely of acknowledging and respecting the right in question' (*Pacem in Terris*).

In addition to the strictly natural rights mentioned above we have the vast field of contingent rights whereby certain things or actions are due to a man on the basis of positive law or private agreement.

In a true sense duties in justice are the most tangible and enforceable of all duties. Whereas the object of the other virtues can be a man's private affair, this can never be said of justice. Justice always involves another. The subject owes something not to himself but to another, and that other can actually compel him to grant it. This is the force of St Thomas's statement that the object of justice is not merely a *debitum morale* but a *debitum legale*. The party has a strict legal title to it and he can vindicate it as his right against all comers.[24]

It has frequently been noted that St Thomas, following his Greek and Roman masters, employs the word *ius* in its objective sense to denote that which is owed, whereas modern theologians

[23] Paulist Press Edition, p. 8.

[24] 'Debitum quidem legale est ad quod reddendum aliquis lege adstringitur; et tale debitum proprie attendit justitia, quae est principalis virtus. Debitum autem morale est quod aliquis debet ex honestate virtutis' (*S. theol.*, II-II, 80, un).

use it in the subjective sense indicating the moral faculty of appropriation and control which a person enjoys in regard to a certain object.[25] Many Thomists deprecate this ' abuse ' of the term and claim that it is a source of confusion.[26] I do not agree. It is undeniable that the two meanings are intimately connected; but to my mind the subjective sense is the more fundamental and is logically prior. The only reason why a given thing or action is a *ius* or *debitum* in the objective sense, is that a certain person has a right to demand or possess it. It is due to him because it is bound to him by some title which gives him an exclusive claim on it. The ultimate reason for an obligation in justice will be found not by analysing the matter but by examining the subject. If we wish to determine whether a given thing is a matter of justice, we look to the title of the claimant. His title may derive from his human nature (the right to life), from a just law (the right to prescribe), from some contingent fact (contract, injury). On foot of this title he can claim something as his own. In other words he has a strict right to it: ' Facultas legitima et exlcusiva et in proprium commodum.'

This personal or subjective approach to the idea of right serves as a corrective to the very material notion of justice suggested by the classical definition of Ulpian: ' Constans et perpetua voluntas ius suum cuique tribuendi' The concept implicit in the idea of handing over something suggests that justice governs mere transactions in external goods, whereas

[25] 'Jus primo impositum est ad significandum ipsam rem iustam' (*Ibid.* II-II, 57, 1 ad 1). 'De nos jours, le terme *ius* revêt deux sens: un sens primitif, ce qui est dû, c'est-a-dire l'objet de la vertu de justice, et un sens dérivé, la faculté inviolable qu'un sujet possède d'orienter cet objet a son avantage. Or on ne voit pas nulle part ce dernier sens subjectif dans la littérature du XIIe et du XIIIe siècle,' (O. Lottin, *Le droit naturel chez saint Thomas d'Aquin et ses prédécesseurs*, Bruges 1931, 97–98). The authority of Suarez' *De Legibus* was in large measure responsible for the general acceptance of the subjective sense: 'Iuxta posteriorem et *strictam* iuris significationem solet proprie ius vocari facultas quaedam moralis quam unusquisque habet circa rem suam, vel ad rem sibi debitam.'

[26] See P.-M. Van Overbeke, O.P., 'Droit et morale,' *Revue Thomiste* 58 (1958), 287–311.

justice exercises its most important function in protecting the human rights to life, to integrity, to freedoms of one kind or another. One is chary about suggesting another definition, but the following would seem to meet the case more satisfactorily. Justice is the moral virtue which inclines one to respect man's personality and to grant him what is due to him as an individual charged with the responsibility of his own destiny.

Equality

For the ancient Pythagorean school of philosophy justice was primarily equality, an equilibrium between extremes. They employed the number eight, 'an evenly even number' (ἀριθμὸς ἰσάκις ἴσος) to express the fact.[27] This metaphorical play on numbers is devoid of any special appeal to the modern mind, but the truth which it aimed to express is basic. Equality is a most obvious value in justice: 'Justitia autem aequalitas quaedam est,' says St Thomas.[28]

Justice establishes equality after a double fashion. Firstly, where it concerns the person as individual, it equates that which he possesses with that to which he has a right. Aristotle, and after him the Scholastics, called this arithmetical equality. It is a simple, elementary computation. A man has a right to a certain determinate amount or to a definite action. His right is satisfied when he obtains this amount or when he is allowed to perform this action. Secondly, as between a number of individuals in reference to a common property or burden, justice establishes equality in that it grants or imposes on each a fair proportion. This is termed geometric equality or an equality of proportion.

The adage, 'Virtus in medio stat,' applies in a particular way to justice. In the other moral virtues the mean is decided purely

[27] 'Pythagorici vero hunc numerum iustitiam vocaverunt: quia primus omnium ita solvitur in numeros pariter pares, hoc est in bis quaterna, ut nihilominus in numeros aeque pariter pares divisio quoque ipsa solvatur, id est in bis bina. Eadem quoque qualitate contexitur, id est bis bina bis' (Macrobius, *Comment. in Somnium Scipionis*, 1, 5, 17–18).

[28] *S. theol.*, I-II, 114, Ic.

by a rational judgment which strikes a middle point between excess and defect in a given sphere. In his own conscience a man decides what he should do in the circumstances. This is a *medium rationis*. In matters of justice, however, the question is decided for him and the decision on the extent of his obligation is taken out of his hands. The requirement of equality between individuals and the existence of a determinate claim to a certain amount decide the measure of action. So the mean of justice is said to be a *medium rei*.[29] This *medium rei* is particularly obvious in the arithmetical equality of commutative justice since this type of justice equates object and object, for example, commodity and price, damage and reparation. The mean is more difficult to establish in the case of distributive justice. Since this aims at a fair distribution of benefits and burdens within the community it must take into account and compare the relative merits and capacities of the members.[30]

THE FORMS OF JUSTICE

The question, how many are the species of justice, has ever been a source of disagreement among philosophers and theologians. With Aristotle [31] and St Thomas [32] we say that justice

[29] 'Cum medium sit quod inter extrema versatur: in moralibus autem extrema sunt plus et minus, excessus et defectus: medium virtutis est illud bonum, quod inter excessum et defectum consistit. Si sola ratio medium illud determinet, secundum qualitatem personae, dicitur medium rationis; si autem constituatur per comparationem rei ad rem, sive per aequalitatem unius rei ad alterum, est medium rei' (Sylvius, *Comment. in Summam S. Thomas*, II-II, q. 58, a. 10).

[30] 'In iustitia distributiva non accipitur medium secundum aequalitatem rei ad rem, sed secundum proportionem rerum ad personas, ut scilicet sicut una persona excedit aliam, ita etiam res quae datur uni personae, excedat rem quae datur alii' (*S. theol.* II-II, 61, 2).

[31] 'One kind is that which has to do with the distribution of honour, wealth and other things that are divided among the members of the body politic (for in these circumstances it is possible for one man's share to be unfair or fair as compared with another's); and another kind is that which has to give redress in private transactions' (*Nic. Eth.* 5, 2, 12).

[32] *S. theol.* II-II, 61, 2.

has two species: commutative and distributive. Commutative justice governs the relations between individuals. It commands each to respect the right of the other, to refrain from undue interference, to honour contracts, to repair injuries. This is the justice of arithmetical equality; the parties encounter one another on an equal footing. On the other hand distributive justice, as its name implies, demands that a fair distribution of the goods and burdens of society be made to all the members on a proportional basis. As one's contribution to the economy is greater one has a right to a greater return; as one's need is more urgent one has a right to greater assistance; as one possesses more wealth one is obliged to bear heavier taxes. Beforehand no one has a strict right to any given benefit or service, but all have a right to demand that the correct order be observed in the distribution of benefits and obligations. This is the guiding principle of the executive authority of the state, of the department which administers the laws of public assistance, grants, taxes, and the rest.

Each of these forms of justice realizes in its own way the three essential qualities: otherness, a right to be satisfied, and equality. In commutative justice the otherness attains the status of an opposition between two individuals who are set over one against the other; the right means that one claims a certain object because it is immediately one's own by some exclusive title; the equality is of the absolute arithmetical form. In distributive justice the otherness is not that of two separate individuals, it is a distinction between parts in the whole; the right is that of claiming a share in a common property; the equality is one of proportion between persons of varying merits or capacities.

Distributive justice is a true species of justice and it possesses the three essential properties. It has been downgraded by a great many theologians following the lead of Billuart, who compared it unfavourably with strict or commutative justice.[33] This was not the view of St Thomas or of Soto, and of other eminent authori-

[33] *Comment. in Summam S. Thomae* tom. 6, disp. 8, art. 1, par. 14.

ties in the field.[34] In their eyes distributive justice was of higher value in that it was the virtue of the head of the community and of the judge, both of whom are charged with the responsibility of making a judgment determining what is just in a given situation.

To the above claim one may object that the obligation of restitution arises only from a violation of commutative justice and, therefore, one must naturally conclude that this is the only strict justice. I question the postulate here. It is universally admitted that a violation of distributive justice may imply *per accidens* a violation of commutative justice and an obligation of restitution. But does a violation of distributive justice in itself impose an obligation of restitution? To my mind the answer must be yes. The members of society have a strict right in justice (*ius ad rem*) to enjoy a fair share of the community goods and to bear no more than their due share of taxes. The extent of this right is determined objectively (the mean of justice is a *medium rei*) by the varying claims and capacities of the individuals involved. If distributive justice is violated, a given person has less than he should have, or he pays more than he should pay. This kind of situation demands restitution. In effect, distributive justice is called on to establish a just balance of proportion between various individuals; commutative justice is called on to re-establish this balance if it has been disturbed. This is undeniably the teaching of St Thomas,[35] Cajetan,[36] Soto,[37] and a number of modern theologians.[38]

[34] See A.-J. Faidherbe, *La justice distributive*, Paris, 1934,: 9 'Saint Thomas fait de grands eloges de cette vertu. Il nous montre en elle la vertu du chef; il indique avec soin son rôle prépondérant en tout judgment et sa supériorité sur la commutative.' In this again St Thomas was loyal to Aristotle, who placed distributive justice higher on the scale than commutative (Note the order in n. 31 above). Soto, *De iustitia et iure*, 2, 5, 1 gives one reason: 'Justitia distributiva utpote quae in principe potissimum praeeminet, qua bona communia singulis civibus adjudicat, praestantior est commutativa.'

[35] *S. theol.* II-II, 62, I, arg. 3 et resp.

[36] *Comment.* in II-II, 62, 6, n. 1.

[37] *Op. cit.*, 4, 6, 1.

[38] For example, J. Dabin, *Théorie générale du droit*, Brussels, 1944, 240; A.-J. Faidherbe, *op. cit.*, 129–39; P.-M. Van Overbeke *art. cit.*, 290–91; D. O'Donoghue, 'The scope of distributive justice,' *Irish Theol. Quart.*, 21 (1954), 303–5.

Faidherbe states as a principle: 'La distributive impose la restitution et la com-

In most of our text-books distributive justice and its correlative vice *acceptio personarum* are dismissed in a few lines. A very little reflection will show the importance of distributive justice on the part of those authorities in the community who have benefits in their gift, or who are called on to portion out burdens and obligations. When the Scriptures speak of injustice, it is usually the injustice of the unfair superior or judge that is in question:

> Thou shalt not do that which is unjust, nor judge unjustly. Respect not the person of the poor, nor honour the countenance of the mighty. But judge thy neighbour according to justice.[39]
>
> There shall be no difference of persons. You shall hear the little as well as the great. Neither shall you respect any man's person because it is the judgment of God.[40]

This iron law of fairness is underlined in a striking manner in the command of *Exodus* 23: 3: 'Thou shalt not favour a poor man in judgment.'

The opportunities for injustice in distribution are multiplied in the modern highly organized society. The organs of national and local government, the civil service, appointments' boards, examiners, arbitrators are expected to make their decisions solely on the objective merits of the candidates for posts, grants, examinations, contracts, awards of one kind or another. How easy it is to allow judgment to be prejudiced by extraneous considerations of family or politics, bribery in money or kind, favour for friend or friend's friend!

mutative l'exécute' (p. 134). On this O'Donoghue comments: 'Once his right is established through the comparison of merits and claims, it becomes absolute, a right which can be held against all others. If it is violated, something definite is taken from him, and justice demands that he receive it back, or its equivalent, but the justice which is in question now has a rectifying function; it is commutative justice' (p. 305).

[39] *Lev.* 19: 15.

[40] *Deut.* 1: 17. See also *Deut.* 10: 17, 16: 19; *Prov.* 18: 5; *Mal.* 2: 9; *Eph.* 6: 9; *Col.* 3: 25.

LEGAL OR GENERAL JUSTICE

In our introductory paragraphs we saw that the Greek philosophers frequently employed the term justice in a wide or general sense. The just man was the good citizen, he who advanced the common interest by doing his duty or that which the law enjoined. To quote Aristotle: 'We apply the term just to whatever tends to produce and preserve the happiness of the community.'[41] St Thomas is loyal to this tradition in his treatment of legal or general justice. It is the virtue of the good citizen, the virtue which directs the acts of all the virtues to the common good.[42] The formal object of this virtue is the common welfare and, since law is the chief means by which the common welfare is achieved, it is also called legal justice, the justice which enjoins obedience to law.[43]

Though this virtue is called justice, it is not a species of the cardinal virtue. Many philosophers claim that it is, but it taxes their ingenuity to identify in it the strict elements of justice. In fact the differences between particular and legal justice are so substantial, that the attempt to make this latter a full partner with the former in the sphere of cardinal justice dilutes the whole notion of justice. Whereas particular justice, commutative or distributive, aims to satisfy the rights of an individual–determined physical or moral person, general justice aims to satisfy the demands of law and of the common welfare;[44] whereas particular justice has a limited object in that it grants each one his strict due, general justice has a general matter in that it directs the acts of all virtues to the common good;[45] the mean of particular justice is always a *medium rei*, the mean of general

[41] *Nic. Eth.* 5, 1, 13.

[42] 'Virtus boni civis est justitia generalis . . . Justitia legalis dicitur esse virtus generalis, in quantum scilicet ordinat actus omnium virtutum ad bonum commune' (*S. theol.* II-II, 58, 6).

[43] *Ibid.* II-II, 58, 5.

[44] *Ibid.* II-II, 70, 3.

[45] 'Iustitia legalis et iniustitia est circa totam materiam moralem' (S. Thomas, *In V. Ethic.*, 1, 3).

justice is a *medium rei* only when it deals with matters of particular justice; otherwise it is a *medium rationis*.

It was mentioned above that the acts of any virtue, for example, truth, courage, temperance, obedience, can be the object of general justice; but it should be noted that acts of commutative and distributive justice are of special moment in this regard. In all legal codes statutes protecting the person, property, and general fair-dealing constitute a major part of legislation; and the external and determined nature of matters of justice makes them particularly suitable for the juridical imperative.

In modern times a new term, social justice, is widely used. The term acquired general recognition through its repeated use in the encyclical *Quadragesimo Anno*. Its exact meaning has puzzled commentators and some have seen in it a new addition to the justice family. In my opinion this multiplication of entities is quite unjustified. In social justice, or justice of the common welfare, it is easy to recognize the general justice of St Thomas. In Pius XI's encyclical *Divini Redemptoris* we come nearest to a definition: 'It is of the very essence of social justice to demand from each individual all that is necessary to the common good.'[46]

Social justice aims to produce a proper social order, it aims to produce those economic, political, moral and intellectual conditions which will allow all the citizens to live a fully human life. Every citizen within his own field is bound to contribute to the common welfare; for example, the wealthy man must consider the social obligations of property and he must use his wealth to further the common good. In a special way this furthering of the common good is a function of government, and consequently distributive justice looms large in the field where social justice operates:

> It is impossible to care for the social organism and the good of society as a unit unless each single part and each individual member is supplied with all that is necessary for the exercise of his social functions.[47]

[46] C.T.S. edition, par. 51. [47] *Ibid.*

JUSTICE AND THE CHRISTIAN

It is easy to see how justice gains a place of honour in a purely humanist philosophy of life. As a principle of order and coexistence it satisfies the legitimate demands of individual and community. At the personal level justice exacts respect for a man's individuality. It recognizes his independence; it protects him from arbitrary interference; it guarantees him security and the liberty to live his own life and to do as he wishes with that which is his. At the community level justice promotes order and tranquillity by delimiting the spheres of influence of the various individual and social units and preventing the clashes which would inevitably occur if everyone simply consulted his own convenience. In the nature of things justice and law are inseparable. The law must reflect the canons of ideal justice if it is to be a human ordinance and to have force in conscience.[48] Then in its turn this law becomes the measure of justice in ordinary human affairs and transactions.[49]

That justice is an essential and benign force in human life cannot be denied, but justice has also its dangers. Whereas it should control the grasping hand of the selfish man by forcing him to take account of the rights of others, it can also be employed as a mailed fist to vindicate mercilessly one's own rights. This is the weakness of blind instinctive justice. Hence the proverbs: 'Summum ius, summa iniuria; ne sis iustus nimis.' In any situation the merely just man defines his position by, 'I am within my rights; pay what you owe.' The Gospel story of the fate of the servant who throttled his helpless debtor warns us that the cold writ of justice does not run in every human situation. Sometimes custom and law favour the extreme view of justice, as in the vendetta or the *lex talionis*: 'Eye for eye, tooth for tooth, wound for wound,' [50] This is the justice of the

[48] 'Est autem ius a iustitia, sicut a matre sua; ergo prius fuit iustitia quam ius' (Accursius, *Glossa Ordinaria* in *Dig.* 1, 1, 1). References to the unwritten laws (ἄγραφοι νόμοι) of justice are found in Sophocles' *Antigone*, and in Aristotle's *Nic. Eth.* 8, 13, 2.

[49] Law is 'regula iustorum et iniustorum' in *Dig.* 1, 3, 2.

[50] *Exod.* 21: 24–5.

mythical Dikê, blind-folded, sword in hand, balancing debt and payment with inexorable decision.

JUSTICE AND CHARITY

In our introductory paragraphs we saw that for the Graeco-Roman philosopher justice was the queen of the virtues. In the Christian theology of life the place of honour goes to charity. This was the force of Christ's reply to the doctor who asked him: 'Which is the great commandment?'[51] Leo XIII underlined this re-evaluation of the hierarchy of the virtues when he spoke of charity as 'Omnium domina et regina virtutum.'[52]

At first blush one might regard justice and charity as opposed. Justice divides, charity unites; justice holds two beings apart in the measure that they are other; charity welds them together so that the other becomes another self. Does this mean that in the Christian order justice is outmoded? The answer, of course, is no. On the contrary, in the Christian life justice acquires not only new motivation, but a new dimension. In natural justice one respects the rights of the other because he is a human being and a person; in Christian justice one respects the other as someone called to share the divine life and the vision of God. Not only does this safeguard the human rights of the other, but it enjoins respect for a right which would otherwise remain undiscovered, the primary right to live a full Christian life and attain one's supernatural end.[53] Therefore, the Christian as a Christian has rights in justice, and he can appeal to a new title when claiming respect for them, the title of brother in Christ. In Christianity the whole quality of justice is altered because

[51] *Matt.* 22: 39. Cf. *John* 13: 34: 'A new commandment I give unto you, that you love one another as I have loved you.'

[52] *Rerum Novarum*, ASS 23 (1890–91), 670.

[53] 'Notons bien ici un point important: ce n'est pas n'importe quel droit d'autrui que nous fera respecter la justice infuse, mais c'est le droit d'autrui à la vie éternelle. Et parceque la vie éternelle répresente un epanouissement de tout l'être en Dieu, le chrétien est, plus que quiconque, soucieux de ne pas frustrer autrui des droits de sa personne, de sa dignité et de ses besoins' (*Initiation Théologique*, Paris, 1953, III, 732).

the Christian subject is a new creature; his purpose in life, the value of his activity, the nature of his liberty are completely new.

Charity is the form of all the other virtues, the force which gives the other virtues their truly Christian sense, and an over-all direction and orientation to the last end.[54] Every virtue is a mediation of charity; it is a reflection of that inner dynamism which is the soul of the Christian life. Each virtue translates the demands of charity in a given field; and, consequently, charity properly understood is the sum-total of all the virtues. But charity does not displace the other virtues; these still preserve their specific nature and value, while they mediate charity in the particular situation. Justice operates between Christians in that they are still individuals with definite rights and responsibilities; but it is now the servant of charity which aims to draw these individuals ever more closely together into a single community in Christ. It is worthy of note that the oft-quoted text of St Paul, 'Charity is the plenitude of the law,' is employed by him to inculcate the precept of justice: 'Render therefore to all men their dues . . . owe no man anything, but love one another. For he that loveth his neighbour has fulfilled the law.'[55] Instead of saying 'Be just,' he says, 'Love one another.' The greater contains the lesser.

Christian charity is no vague benevolence which dispenses with definite demands; it is no talisman or super-virtue which licenses one to ignore more 'limited' duties. These duties receive their specifically Christian sense from charity. They are carried along as it were in a current of charity; but charity depends upon them for its effectiveness. Respect for the virtue of justice guarantees the minimum conditions and foundations of charity. Its function is to make love possible.[56]

[54] 'Charitas omnium virtutum forma est cum per ipsam omnium virtutum actus ad debitum et ultimum finem ordinantur' (*S. theol.* II-II, 23, 8).

[55] *Rom.* 13: 7–10.

[56] Gillemann, following Carpentier, suggests the following definition of justice: 'The moral virtue which causes us to respect the person of our brother in Christ, at least in what concerns his rights, in view of assuring between us the minimum of relations that is necessary for union in charity' (*The Primacy of Charity in Moral Theology*, London, 1959, 341).

It is clear, then, that charity does not supersede justice. It carries to ultimate completion the work which it initiates in justice; it does not rest satisfied with the minimum required by right or law; it thinks only of the need of the neighbour. By this very fact it is an important corrective for possible abuses of justice. Instinctive justice, as we already remarked, often masquerades as authentic virtue. The subject of a grievance will father his unreasonable demands or disordered reactions on an allegedly legitimate desire to see justice done. The vindictiveness and resentment which accompany it show that we are dealing here with a disordered instinct. The antidote to this is charity; it breathes an atmosphere which surrounds justice and defends it from itself: 'Charity is patient, is kind . . . is not ambitious, seeketh not her own, is not provoked to anger, thinketh no evil.'[57] The Christian will be scrupulous in respecting the rights of his brother in Christ; but he will show condescension and restraint in the matter of his own rights. No wonder this doctrine was a scandal to the Jews and folly to the Gentiles:

> You have heard that it was said 'Eye for eye' and 'Tooth for tooth.' But I tell you, do not resist the evildoer. Nay whosoever smites you on your right cheek, turn to him the other also. And to him that would go to law with you and take your tunic, give up your cloak also. And whosoever compels you to go one mile, go with him two.[58]

A THEOLOGY OF JUSTICE

It is true that the approach to justice in our traditional moral manuals can be faulted on a number of counts. It has been said, for example, that the justice tract is not much more than a course in natural law, that it leans too heavily on the method and matter of positive legislation, that it luxuriates in casuistry.

The complaint that the justice tract is not much more than a

[57] 1 *Cor.* 13: 4–5.
[58] *Matt.* 5: 38–41.

course in natural law has some foundation. The fault can be traced to St Thomas himself. He borrowed from Aristotle not only the terms and technical elements in the concept of justice, but also the appreciation and background of the virtue. He analyses in minute detail the various factors in natural justice and the similarities and distinctions between it and other virtues. Though in a previous section of the *Summa* he has demonstrated that charity is the form of the virtues, he fails to make any application of that in his questions on justice.

The justice tract must take account of the natural law elements which we analysed at the beginning. These are basic if one is to have any concrete, scientific idea of the virtue's nature and sphere of action. But it must be remembered that for the Christian natural justice is not enough. The quality of just relations is completely altered because of his appreciation of what his neighbour really is. The claims of justice become the claims of love. Perhaps over-emphasis on a mere natural justice explains the paradox of the Christian who blandly claims that 'he is within his rights,' even though his action or lack of action is likely to harm others. In mere justice the Good Samaritan could have passed by the robbers' victim claiming 'Neminem laedit qui suo iure utitur.' But the Christian must always act responsibly, and responsibility means taking account of the total situation. No one has the right to abuse his property or his power on the plea that it is his own. Sometimes justice is defined as 'the right to use and *abuse* what is one's own to the extent permitted by law.' This is based on a quite erronous translation of Ulpian's 'ius utendi et abutendi re sua, quatenus iuris ratio patitus.' In the context *abutendi* means 'to use up.'

The Christian generosity of the Sermon on the Mount is much more demanding than the cold measure of legal rights and obligations; but it must be remembered that respect for these rights and duties is a first essential step towards that ideal. Attaining this first rung on the ladder of Christian perfection can be quite a step. The prevalence of theft, irresponsible debts, unfair business practices cannot be ignored. A moral or pastoral theology which would omit a detailed consideration of these would not be realistic.

It is also urged against the traditional justice tract that it leans too heavily on law, that it glorifies law as the criterion of justice. True, law has always enjoyed an undoubted prominence in matters of justice. In both the Greek and Hebrew traditions justice was established when the prince and judge imposed and interpreted the law well and equitably, and when the citizens observed it conscientiously. 'The law seeks to establish that which is just and proper and beneficial, and its statute is fair and equitable to all,' says Demosthenes.[59] St Thomas saw law and justice in the same light. He defines the object of justice in terms of law: 'Debitum legale, ad quod reddendum aliquis lege adstringitur.'[60]

It would be a sad day for both law and justice if the attempt to separate them succeeded. Their inter-relation is not to be dismissed simply as a historical fact; it is based on the nature of things. It is the function of justice to introduce order and reason into human affairs; law proposes to itself an identical task.[61] A law which is not inspired by justice is simply not a law, whereas a law which is just and reasonable actually determines the extent of one's rights and duties in justice.

Admitting that law has a place in the justice tract, does not mean that one endorses the prominence heretofore given to it. The medieval moralists loaded their texts with references to the Roman Corpus and to the Decretals. In many cases they saw no need to press their enquiries beyond the positive law, and one marvels at their ingenuity in quoting law to their purposes. Their formation and outlook were so coloured by law, that their texts could pass as legal tracts. This tradition was maintained

[59] *Contra Aristogeiton*, 4, 2.

[60] *S. theol.* II-II, 80, un. Cf. I, 16, 4 ad 3: 'Veritas iustitiae est secundum quod home servat id quod debet alteri secundum ordinem legum.'

[61] 'Ad ipsam (iustitiam) pertinet ordinem rationis ponere in omnibus rebus humanis' (*Ibid.* II-II, 123, 12). 'Lex est quaedam rationis ordinatio ad bonum commune' (*Ibid.* I-II, 90, 4).

to modern times, and may be seen at its most extreme in specialized works such as those of Crolly and Carriére. The solution to this problem is to be found simply in a proper sense of proportion, which will give the more important biblical and theological aspects their true value.

Our traditional justice tract has also been faulted because of the extent to which it indulges in casuistry. True, many of the classical casus have nothing to recommend them apart from the opportunity they afford for an ingenious play of principles; they tend to give an air of unreality to the whole discussion. But the objection to casuistry often goes much deeper than this, suggesting that the moralist has no right to intervene at the level of actual moral decision. Every situation is so unique, that the only person who is entitled to judge is the agent himself. The casuist tends to distort the position in that he proposes to apply a general norm without a proper appreciation of the circumstances. This is not the place for a discussion on absolute moral values or on the extent to which circumstances alter cases; but it can be said that the moralist who would simply air the principles and then 'leave it to each one's conscience' to apply them in real life, does not give much guidance. Indeed, he may well be evading the issue. True, he may not remove from people the responsibility of moral decision; but he must show the principles which are operative, and how they affect the decision in a given case. The well-chosen casus can do this admirably, In this he is following in the footsteps of the Master who 'taught in parables.'[62]

[62] The case for casuistry is well stated by E. Hamel, S.J.: 'Valeur et limites de la casuistique,' *Sciences Ecclésiastiques*, 11 (1959) 147–73.

SIN AND REPENTANCE

Cornelius Williams, O.P.

It can, I think, be maintained without exaggeration that in the matter of sin and its remission there is today unfortunately a widespread misunderstanding among theologians and great confusion among the Christian people. That was made abundantly clear in the now notorious *Honest to God* debate, in which so many of the participants, including Dr Robinson himself, showed themselves to have quite false notions of God and, as a necessary consequence, utterly false notions of sin which were based ultimately on erroneous conceptions of love and divine charity. It is almost a truism to say that where there is no real sense of God there can be no true sense of sin. Perhaps of all the tracts in moral theology that on sin is the most difficult and intricate; and for that very reason it is either omitted completely or given such a perfunctory and superficially legalistic treatment that confusion and misunderstanding rather than clarification is thereby engendered. And for all that, the tract on sin is from a certain point of view, especially today, one of the most important both from a purely theological (and, I might add, speculative), and from a specifically practical and pastoral point of view.[1] There are so many strange and positively false notions prevalent about sin and punishment for sin, about

[1] Sin is a central theme in both the Old and the New Testament and has a very prominent place in every manual of practical moral theology. One of the most penetrating studies of sin from a speculative point of view has been given us in recent years by Alexander M. Horvath, *Heiligkeit und Sünde im Lichte der thomistischen Theologie* (Thomistische Studien 1), Fribourg, Switzerland, 1943.

sorrow for sin and its remission, that a thorough re-thinking of the theology of sin has become one of the most urgent concerns of moral theology. In recent years, in fact, both psychologists and theologians, Catholic and non-Catholic alike, have devoted much time and energy to a re-assessment of its meaning and importance.[2] For a long time sin had become, and perhaps still is in many circles, a most unfashionable word. On the one hand, analytical psychologists were wont to scoff at the idea of sin and the sense of sin and culpability, insisting on the deleterious effects of such conceptions on mental health. On the other hand, sin has become an unpopular word in the minds of those dedicated to the life of the spirit and vowed to the pursuit of Christian perfection. It seems to be forgotten that one of the most important elements in the pursuit of Christian perfection is precisely the eradication from our lives of sin and all its remnants. And that is the work of a lifetime. Ascetical and mystical theology, we are told, deals with the life of Christian perfection and the means towards its attainment; moral theology, mere moral theology, busies itself with the life of the sinner, with sin in all its manifestations. In that sense moral theology, as distinct from ascetical and mystical theology, has been most unfortunately reduced to being a science of sin or, in another form which brings out the soul-killing legalistic approach to the Christian life found in all too many books on moral theology, it is reduced to being a science of the licit and the illicit, of that which is according to or against the law.[3] It would almost appear

[2] The following recent works may be noted: *Thêologie du Péché*, at Pastorale du Péché (Bibliothèque de Théologie, série II, Théologie Morale, vol. 7 and 8), Desclee & Co., Tournai, 1960 (collective work); *Le Péché* (coll. Présence Chrétienne), Desclée de Brouwer, Paris, 1959 (collective work); Henri Rondet, *Notes sur la theologie du péché*, Paris, 1957; Jérôme Regnier, *Der moderne Mensch und die Sünde*, Würzburg, 1959. At the annual convention of the American Psychological Association in September 1959 the central theme for discussion was: The Rôle of the Concept of Sin in Psychotheraphy. And in August of the same year the main topic of discussion at the evangelical *Kirchentag* held in Munich was sin and confession.
[3] Cf. H. Davis, *Moral and Pastoral Theology*, I, 4; T. Slater, *Cases of Conscience*, I, 36; C. Williams, " The Meaning of Morals," *Doctrine and Life*, 10 (1960) 70–76.

that moral theology has nothing more to do than to determine the exact limits between mortal and venial sin in order to be in a position to show people how far they may go without incurring eternal punishment and going to hell, or in order to show them how to scrape into heaven by hook or by crook! That is unfortunately more or less the state of affairs against which, in recent times, many theologians are rightly re-acting and for which they are exerting every effort to find a remedy.[4]

SIN AND THE CHRISTIAN LIFE

The Christian life is something much more noble and beautiful than one devoted to the avoiding of mortal sin at all costs. That is a purely negative approach to life and is ultimately destructive of all true progress in the spiritual life. The Christian life is not a life led in the fear of punishment, but rather one flowing from the love of and the enthusiasm for an ideal, that ideal being conformity to Christ in life and action. That is true not only of those who by profession are dedicated to a life of perfection, but also of all Christians who are called by Christ to follow him and learn of him. 'Come to me,' he says, 'all you that labour and are burdened; I will give you rest. Take my yoke upon yourselves, and learn of me; I am gentle and humble of heart; and you will find rest for your souls. For my yoke is easy, and my burden is light.'[5] Christianity is an élan coming from within, and not a juridically coloured moral system. With joy and gladness Christians are called to set themselves to follow in the footsteps of their Master. 'You are to be perfect, as your heavenly Father is perfect'[6] is our Lord's injunction to all his disciples and not just to a small chosen group of specially dedicated souls.

Christian morality is not based on the structure and exigencies

[4] I refer to the excellent work done in this line by theologians like Hirscher, Tillmann, Häring, Gillemann etc.

[5] *Matt.* 11:28–30

[6] *Matt.* 5:48.

of human nature alone, but on the word or revelation of God, our Creator. It is important, then, to recall here the double aspect of faith which is often either misunderstood or totally neglected. Faith, we may say quite simply, means taking God as his word; it means taking Christ, God made man, at his word. It is, to put the matter another way, man's answer to God's revealing word. However, we must ever keep in mind that God spoke to men and entered into that mysterious personal contact with them, not just to reveal to them a set of sublime truths which would otherwise ever remain hidden to the mind of man;[7] faith is more than that, for God spoke to man for another reason; and I am inclined to think that this other reason is in fact the principal one.[8] God spoke to man in order to teach him how to live, in order to bring him to a consciousness of his dignity as a child and friend of God, made according to his image and likeness, called to share in a supreme degree in the life and blessedness of God in the vision of heaven. 'Blessed are the clean of heart; they shall see God,'[9] is the solemn promise and declaration of our Lord himself. God spoke to men, too, in order to show them the obstacles in the path to perfection, in order to warn them of the dangers that lie in the way of the growth or development of divine life within them; in other words, in order to impress upon them the real and tragic meaning of sin. For sin, in that light, appears as something which impedes or even stifles completely growth in Godlikeness and Christlikeness; it appears as something barring our way to heaven, our entry into the kingdom of God, and rendering impossible that sharing in God's own life which has its culmination in the vision of heaven to which all

[7] Cf. Vatican I, sess. 3, cap. 4, *Denz.* 3016.

[8] I refer here to the revelation of a new morality and to faith precisely as practical and to the declaration of our Lord: 'I have come so that they may have life, and have it more abundantly' (*John* 10: 10).

[9] *Matt.* 5: 8. The doctrine of the beatific vision is of supreme importance in the whole fundamental and moral theology. It is also basic to a proper understanding of the true notion of the supernatural. Consequently it is of great interest to note that this text of Matthew is the only one in which our Lord himself promises the vision of God to those who are pure of heart, that is, to those who are purified

men are called, and into which all men, leading their daily lives according to the will of God and the teaching and example of Christ, are invited to grow.[10]

I have said that men are called *to grow into* the glory of heaven; for here we are dealing with the growth or development of a free creature, composed of body and spirit and endowed with freewill and reason, into full maturity. And as distinct from the growth of lower animate beings the growth and development of man precisely as a human being is in his own hands; it is his own work and for it he has full responsibility.[11] If he fosters and cares for this life then it will flourish and finally blossom into the life of glory, into eternal life which is the crowning of this life on earth.[12] Now God has spoken to us in order to tell us most concretely how to live and act in order to arrive one day at this fullness of being.[13] and also in order to tell us what kind of life and action will kill or stifle this growth and thus exclude from the kingdom of heaven.[14] Whatever stifles or retards this development is obviously harmful and evil; it is sinful and

and sanctified by the moral virtues and by perfect submission to the will of God the Father in heaven; that is the one essential condition for the obtaining of the Beatific Vision. However, this solemn promise (made in the Sermon on the Mount) of our Lord must have made a most profound impression on his hearers and on all the subsequent authors of the New Testament; for exegetes admit that when they speak of the Beatific Vision they have these words and this promise of our Lord in mind (cf. 1 *Cor.* 13: 12; *Heb.* 12: 14; 1 *John* 3: 2; *Apoc.*22: 4–5). Another matter of the greatest importance, and one forgotten or just not understood by exegetes and theologians alike, is the following: the supernatural character of the vision of God can be demonstrated by reason alone. And here we have the one solid foundation for our whole theology of the supernatural.

[10] Cf. St Thomas, *S. theol.*, I, II, 6, prol.

[11] Cf. St Thomas, *S. theol.*, I, II, 1, 2. And in this connection one should consult A.-I. Mennessier, *Saint Thomas d'Aquin* (coll. Les Maîtres de la Spiritualité Chrétienne, Textes et Etudes), pp. 44–56.

[12] This is the real meaning of St Thomas's whole tract on beatitude (*S. theol.*, I, II, 1–5). It is ultimately the meaning too of the definition of faith found in *Heb.* 11: 1.

[13] This is an expression of St Thomas himself in *De Ver.* 22.7.

[14] See the lists of sins or vices given by St Paul in *Rom.* 1: 29–32 and *Gal.* 5: 19–21. All the sins or vices enumerated exclude from the kingdom of heaven.

precisely in the degree in which it stifles or impedes our spiritual growth. It is the duty of each one to promote that growth with every care and sedulously avoid whatever is harmful to it. In saying that we are a long way from a legalistic or purely juridical notion of sin. We are in the domain of life and organic progress. All life it must be said, is governed by certain laws, the laws of life, which must be rigorously observed. It is obvious that even the growth of a plant, for instance a rose-tree, is governed by certain laws; and the gardener owes it to himself and to the plant to heed these laws, otherwise there will be no blooms to delight him with their beauty and fragrance.

It should be fairly obvious that we are dealing here with law in a very special sense, in a sense that is in one way known to all, but in another is almost completely neglected; and that is the case, most unfortunately, in moral theology as taught and expounded especially in the Western Church since the seventeenth century.[15] We are dealing with law not imposed from without, curbing or at least limiting and ordering the innate freedom of individuals in the context of social life, but rather postulated by the very structure of human being and flowing from within, just as the law that governs the growth of the rose-tree flows from the very nature of the plant itself. Even when formulated in instructions and principles of action, this inner law does not cease to be the law of growth and perfection, the price paid for its breach being nothing more nor less than the dwarfing or stunting of the nature of which it is the law. God's moral law as manifested in Sacred Scripture and as handed down to and interpreted for us by the teaching authority of the Church, is the law of our being.[16] Its transgression will inevitably bring

[15] Cf. Anon., 'D'une thérapeutique spirituelle du scrupule,' *La Vie Spirituelle, Supplément*, March19 35, p. 141–153. In this connection many interesting insights may be found in N. Berdyaev's *The Destiny of Man*, in the chapter on hell, 266–83, London, 1954; but one will not agree with everything the author has to say.

[16] In this connection one could profitably read the three questions which St Thomas devoted to an analysis of the nature and structure of the New Law (*S. theol.*, I, II, 106–8). The following significant statement is found in the very first article :

about the diminution of ourselves as human beings, as divinized human beings made to the image of God and called to be his children and his friends.[17] When dealing with God's moral law, then, we have to do not with a kind of police law but rather with our Maker's instructions.[18]

Here another matter of paramount importance for a true understanding of sin and its punishment should be noted. Just as for the faithful observance of God's law, the law of our Christian being, we are promised by God the reward of eternal life (into which, as we saw, from another point of view, we grow and develop; but since the whole supernatural and Christian life from beginning to end is grace, therefore its culmination in eternal life may rightly be considered as a reward given by God), so we are threatened with eternal damnation in hell, if we do not observe that law.[19] This is certainly a frightening consideration, and especially so if we fail to grasp its true theological meaning and instead think of God as a hard and harsh task-master ever watching for our failings and misdemeanours in order to punish us accordingly, and not as a loving father and friend who has only our good at heart. Even a simple consideration of God as Creator should bring that fact home to us. God did not make things outside himself and give them a sharing in his own being and goodness and perfection in the sure knowledge that they would inevitably go to their destruction; much less did he ordain them to such a destruction. It is unthinkable, then, that God should have created man, that image of himself endowed with

Id autem quod est potissimum in lege novi testamenti, et id in quo virtus eius consistit, est gratia Spiritus Sancti, quae datur per fidem Christi . . . Et ideo dicendum est quod principaliter nova lex est lex indita, secundario autem est lex scripta (*loc. cit.*, q. 106, art. 1).

[17] Cf. St Thomas, *II Sent.* dist. 34, q. 1, art. 3: *Operationes morales non sunt factiones ut per eas aliquid in materia constituatur, sed sunt actiones in ipsis agentibus permanentes et eos perficientes aut corrumpentes.* Also III CG cap. 12 in fine; in Anal. Patr. I, lect. 41, n. 7.

[18] The expression and analogy is from F. J. Sheed, *Man: The Forgotten*, London, 1948, 34.

[19] Cf. *Matt.* 25: 31 ff. Also N. Berdyaev, *op. et loc. cit.*

spirit and freedom, if he foresaw that man would inevitably destroy and damn himself; much less did he ordain man to that damnation and destruction. In the last analysis we are forced to admit that damnation is the work of man himself; and that expressed negatively damnation means nothing more nor less than failure to attain to one's final end, to final beatitude and bliss, to eternal life, but relegation instead to everlasting misery and death. For there is, in fact, a double aspect to punishment for sin. Punishment is first and foremost a consequence, a necessary and inevitable consequence of sin. Sin brings with it its own punishment, which consists precisely in a real diminution of human being, a real deformation of God's image in us, a real objective lessening of Godlikeness and Christlikeness in our lives and actions.[20] Whether we like it or not that is the ineluctable effect of our refusal to keep the law of our Maker. Not even our Maker himself can change that.[21] If we fail to observe the maker's instructions about the proper method of using, say, a car or vacuum cleaner, we know what will happen. We cannot blame the maker when through our own negligence these things cease to give us satisfaction, cease to serve us and to function smoothly and efficiently. In this sense theologians rightly speak of the *concommitant* penalty of sin based as it is on the very nature of things.[22]

But over and above that there is another aspect of that same penalty, which attains its deepest and most terrifying point in eternal death or damnation. It is also a penalty rightly and justly

[20] Cf. St Thomas, *S. theol.* I, II, 86, 1, where St Thomas distinguishes a double *nitor rationis*, and shows how sin lessens this *nitor* or *refulgentia naturalis rationis* or *divini luminis* (*scilicet sapientiae et gratiae*).

[21] Cf. St Thomas, *S. theol.* I, II, 71, 6 ad 4. One must carefully distinguish between actions that are evil only because they are forbidden (for instance, eating meat on Friday) and those that are evil on themselves and for that reason are forbidden. We shall see more about this point later on.

[22] Cf. L. Billot, *De personali et originali peccato*, Rome, 1931, 76 ff. Also St Thomas, *II Sent.* dist. 5, q. 2, art. 2 ad 1; *IV Sent.* dist. 18, q. 1, art. 2, qla 1 corp. and ad 4; *QDisp. de Malo*, q. 1, art. 4, ad 5. This notion is also found very frequently in Sacred Scripture.

imposed or inflicted (*poena inflicta vel infligenda*) by God as a result of sin permitted by him and freely committed by us. For we are, in the truest and most literal sense of the term, responsible to God for our own perfection, for our own completion in being, for our own happiness and beatitude, through which and in which we give greatest glory to God our Maker.[23] If we fail to bring ourselves to that perfection in being and life we take away from God's glory and in that sense rightly and justly deserve the punishment that he metes out to us.

BREACH OF GOD'S LAW

Sin has been defined and still is defined in our catechisms as any wilful thought, word, deed or omission contrary to the law of God. This is a definition taken ultimately from St Augustine,[24] accepted and expounded most ingeniously by St Thomas,[25] and handed down to every succeeding generation of Christians. In itself this definition is absolutely correct and corresponds exactly to the notion of sin as found in the accounts of divine revelation in Sacred Scripture and Tradition.[26] But to what great misunderstanding has it not given rise! To what an erroneous conception of the Christian life, which should be one of freshness, newness and enthusiasm, has it not afforded the occasion! Falsely understood in the narrow legalistic sense of human man-made law it has been, perhaps, the source of our present-day legalistic approach in the whole of moral theology.[27] Properly understood, however, in the sense expounded above, in the sense,

[23] Cf. St Thomas, *S. theol.*, I, 103, 2. Also A. Horvath, *Heiligkeit und Sünde*, 144, note 1 and 2.

[24] St Augustine, *Contra Faustum*, lib. 22, ch. 27, PL 42/418.

[25] St Thomas, *S. theol.*, I, II, 71, 6.

[26] See, for instance, the article on sin (Sünde) in the *Bibel-Lexikon* edited by H. Haag, Zürich-Köln, 1951; or special studies to be found in the literature mentioned above in note 2.

[27] See note 3 above. One has only to advert to the fact that the very essence of Catholic life is so frequently seen in the observance of the Sunday precept and abstinence from meat on Friday!

namely, of our Maker's instructions, in the sense of the law of our supernatural and Christian being, it does give us a true insight into the stark reality of sin as a diminution of our own being and as an offence against God who has made us and loves us as a father and as a friend.

Even the very current notion of sin as an offence against God has been misinterpreted in a much too anthropomorphic sense. God cannot be offended as a human being is offended. He is not in that sense susceptible and touchy and easily hurt. Chesterton in his own inimitable way has written the following in this connection: "I could give many (other) examples of words which were right in their Latin use, but which have become obscured in their English misuse. I always feel it in the necessarily frequent phrase 'offending' God; which had originally almost the awful meaning of wounding God. But the word has degenerated through its application to man, until the sound of it is quite petty and perverted. We say that Mr Binks was quite offended or that Aunt Susan will take offence; and lose sight of the essential truth, and even dogma that (in that lower sense) God is the very last to take offence."[28] I should like to quote two obiter dicta (which so often give us such a penetrating insight into the real mind of a man) of St Thomas who, more than any other theologian, has given us a most masterly analysis of sin both from the psychological and from the strictly theological point of view.[29] In one place he says most judiciously that God is never offended unless we do harm to ourselves[30] and in another he warns us against the great danger of determining what is or what is not a mortal sin when there is no true evidence of the fact.[31] When we read and meditate on these observations of the Doctor Communis and recognize their well-founded truth, we begin to breathe freely again and see

[28] G. K. Chesterton, *The Thing* (ed. The Ark Library), 196–7, London, 1938.
[29] Cf. St Thomas, *S. theol.*, I, II, qq. 71–89.
[30] St Thomas, *CG* III, ch. 122, edit. Marietti, n° 2948.
[31] St Thomas, *Q Quodlib.* 9, art. 15. See the judicious remarks of R. Schnackenburg, *Die sittliche Botschaft des Neuen Testaments*, Munich, 1962, 280.

ourselves at last liberated from the intolerable burden of casuistic legalism.

St Thomas has, as I hinted above, given us a most subtle, penetrating and exhaustive analysis of sin. When he comes to determine the real distinction between mortal and venial sin, he is very far from doing so in a narrowly legalistic or casuistic way. For him mortal sin is a human action which breaks the bonds of divine charity and disrupts the ties of friendship that bind us to our Maker, our Father and Friend, and unite us in love to our neighbour, who is also a child and a friend of God.[32] It must, however, be carefully noted here that charity, in the true theological and scriptural sense of the term, is not some sentimental feeling towards God and our neighbour; charity is manifested rather in loyal service and obedience with a view to eternal life. 'If you have any love for me,' said our Lord to his disciples, 'you must keep the commandments which I give you.'[33] And again, perhaps even more strikingly still, he insists: 'The kingdom of heaven will not give entrance to every man who calls me Master, Master; only to the man that does the will of my Father who is in heaven.'[34] Charity, then, quite simply and practically means the keeping of God's law and the law of the Church founded by him for the salvation and sanctification of men.[35] This, as is manifest, is the authentic teaching of Sacred

[32] Cf. *De Malo*, q. 7, art. 1; *S. theol.*, I, II, 87, 3; I, II, 88 *per totum*. Theologians today distinguish between mortal and venial sins and leave it at that. For them, what is not a mortal sin is a venial sin and vice versa. In fact, however, the matter is not at all so simple. Even abstracting from the imperfection of the human act (through lack of knowledge or full consent or defective attention) a distinction, which was made by some of the Church's greatest theologians, seems to have been completely forgotten. Venial sin is of very many kinds and degrees and may consequently be divided into grave and light venial sin. See, for instance, Cajetan in his *Summula Peccatorum*, under *Clericorum peccata*, towards the end of the section. Cf. *S. theol.*, I, II, 73, 2.

[33] *John* 14: 15.

[34] *Matt.* 7: 21.

[35] This teaching is so obviously contained in Sacred Scripture and so clearly to be found in the whole of tradition and in itself most manifest, that St Thomas did not think it necessary to insist on it more than just stating the fact. However, for the interest of the example given, see what he has to say in *S. theol.*, II, II, 168, 3 corp. *in fine*.

Scripture. And we may complete it by saying that our love for God and our keeping of his law are proved to be genuine only if we truly love our neighbour; and our love for our neighbour is truly supernatural and Christian only if we are sincerely active in loving our enemies and those who offend us.[36] The gentle apostle, St John, has put this truth in a most impressive and graphic way when he wrote in his first epistle: 'If a man boasts of loving God, while he hates his own brother, he is a liar. He has seen his brother, and has no love for him; what love can he have for the God he has never seen? No, this is the divine command that has been given us: the man who loves God must be one who loves his brother as well.' [37]

AVERSIO AND CONVERSIO

Up to the present I have attempted to give a rather non-technical description of the scriptural and theological notion of sin. Before passing on, however, to consider repentance, which is the only means whereby the harm done by sin can be made good, I think that a brief technical analysis of sin as a turning away from God (*aversio*) and a turning to created goods in preference to God (*conversio*) is called for. In that way we will be in a better position to understand all the better the true meaning of repentance and all it entails.

Let me begin by saying that as far as I can see there are two fundamental ways of considering sin: either from a purely philosophical point of view or from a specifically theological stand-point.[38] Thus Aristotle has many interesting things, and some very strange things as well, to say about sin and the sinner, about vice and the vicious man. His was a kind of humanist optimism which brought him to imagine that by one's own efforts one could eliminate altogether from one's life sin and all

[36] Cf. *Matt.* 5: 43–44. Also St Thomas, *III Sent.* dist. 30, q. 1, art. I ad 4, and especially *QDisp. de Caritate*, q. 1, art. 8.

[37] 1 *John* 4: 20–21.

[38] Cf. St Thomas. II, *CG*, ch. 4.

traces of it.[39] Here there is no question of reference to the deity or to the gods. Aristotle is interested only in the perfection and completion of man in human goodness through virtue and ultimately through contemplation, which according to him is the crowning of all virtue and supposes virtue already solidly established in the soul. For a theologian, on the other hand, the point of view is totally different. It should be noted in passing that St Thomas was writing as a theologian wherever he discourses on the nature of sin and vice. From beginning to end the theologian considers sin in direct relation to God, as a transgression of his holy will. That is, the theologian considers sin in the context of what the moderns like to call the person-to-person relationship between man, the individual man, and God, creator, law-giver and father.

Now, in the field of theological discussion itself there are also two ways of considering sin. For theology takes as its starting-point the principles of faith accepted on God's word. With regard to the reality of sin the first consideration of the theologian would be to find out exactly what God has said, what exactly he has told us about sin and what actions he has told us are sinful, harmful to ourselves and obstacles to our growth into full completion in human being, which attains full maturity in the kingdom of God in heaven and in the beatific vision of God. In passing it should be carefully noted here that the vision of God has a double function to fulfil: first of all, to unite us to God, the objective extrinsic final end of all things and in a special way of rational and spiritual creatures; and secondly, to constitute us in a state of completion in human being, in the fullness of human life, in the fullness of supernatural life, in the fullness of Godlikeness and Christlikeness.[40] How does one determine exactly what God has said? This is done through the magisterium, either solemn or ordinary, of the Church; through the voice of tradition expressed in these very same Church documents and

[39] Cf. R.-A. Gauthier, *La Morale d'Aristote*, PUF, Paris, 1958, ch. 4.

[40] Cf. St Thomas, *S. theol.*, I, II, 3, 2 ad 2; *IV Sent.* dist. 49, q. 1, art. 2, qla 2 ad 1; *III CG*, ch. 37.

witnessed in the works of the fathers; and in the words of Sacred Scripture itself scrutinized carefully for their true literal sense.

The second consideration of the theologian concerning sin would be something like this. Granted that sin is what it is said to be in the teaching of the Church and in the sources of God's word, what is the reason for it? Surely God does not command or forbid things according to mere whim or fancy? If certain actions are commanded by God, then these actions must of themselves be intrinsically good and conducive to good; and if he forbids certain actions, then these actions must of themselves be intrinsically evil and conducive to the diminution or even the destruction of true human goodness and dignity.[41] It is the theologian's job, then, to find out why some actions are forbidden by the law of God, and why some others are commanded. A theologian will never be satisfied with simply saying, this or that is forbidden or commanded, and that's the end of it! There is no denying that for the faithful, for the believing Christian people, in the ordering of their daily lives, the most important thing, and perhaps the only thing required, is to know with certainty that God has in fact forbidden or commanded this or that. But for the theologian (and by that I mean every priest, especially those who have the care of souls) that is not enough. He must look for the reasons and be in a position, when asked, to give the reasons for the faith that is in him. Today not only in the sphere of dogmatic teaching but also, and perhaps more urgently, in the domain of moral doctrine, people put the question why. Obviously they have a perfect right to do so, and consequently they have a perfect right to expect an answer from us theologians. In looking for the reasons of things the theologian is doing the work proper to theology, I mean, one of the works proper to theology, in making full use of his God-given reason. It was

[41] Cf. the list of sins and vices given by St Paul, note 14 above. Cajetan writes very much to the point: *Lex divina . . . nullum praeceptum pure morale continet nisi de actibus ex genero suo bonis aut malis* (*Comm. in S. theol.*, II, II, 153, 2, edit. Leonina n° XIII).

St Augustine who pointed out to a certain anti-intellectual friend of his (Consentius) this fundamental obligation of every theologian worth the name: *ut ea quae fidei firmitate tenes etiam rationis luce conspicias.*[42] Later St Anselm was to define the work of theology (but be it noted, not the only work of theology) as *fides quaerens intellectum.*[43] These then are the two essential tasks of every theologian, the two essential functions of theology: first of all to find out what exactly God has revealed to man, and secondly, to ask the question why. We might call this double function of investigating and judging the sapiential and the scientific functions of theology respectively.[44]

As regards the problem of sin under discussion I would venture to say that in the context of the sapiential function of theology sin appears first and foremost as a transgression of God's law, and in that sense too a going against his holy will. That is where sin, that is, moral evil, begins and has its origin namely in a wilful, voluntary breach of God's law manifested to man either naturally (that is, through the exigencies of human rational nature itself) or supernaturally by revelation. There we have that first and most important element of all sin in the eyes of a theologian, the turning away from God's law and consequently from God himself, or, in other words, aversion from God. However, since every human action is, of its very essence, a tendency towards something, a concretization of the fundamental appetite of his being towards completion in being, towards real or apparent good, then sin must also appear as a turning towards some good outside God and contrary to his law. It is a turning towards either a merely sensual good, or towards some kind of specious rational good, by-passing, as it were, and neglecting the good as prescribed in God's law, in the instructions of our Maker.[45] There we have the material element of sin, the conversion.

[42] St Augustine, Epist. 120, PL 33/453.
[43] St Anselm, *Proslogion*, proemium, in fine, ed. Schmitt, *op. omn.*, vol. 1, 94.
[44] For this whole matter see F. P. Muniz, *The Work of Theology*, Washington, 1958.
[45] Cf. St Thomas, *S. theol.*, I, II, 6, 4 ad 3; II, II, 130, 1; *QDisp. de Malo*, q. 2, art. 11 ad 13; *ibid.* q. 8, art. 2 ad 12; *IV Sent.* dist. 16, q. 3, art. 2, qla 1 ad 2; *in II Phys.* lect. 8, n° 427–8.

To go a step further and consider the problem in the context of the scientific function of sacred theology we get quite a different, but by no means contrary or opposite view of things. Here the theologian, who already knows with absolute certainty, with the firmness and certainty of faith (*fidei firmitate* of St Augustine) what sin is, strives to find the rational explanation of all that, *ut rationis luce ea quae sunt fidei conspiciat* as St Augustine would put it. His scientific investigation is based on and motivated by the reflexion I made above. God in his moral law commands nothing that is not intrinsically good and salutary, and forbids nothing that is not intrinsically evil. I mean that actions are not good or evil because God commands or forbids them; but that of their very nature they either bring the nature of man, the individual acting human person, to fullness of being and human life and, needless to say, to the fullness of God's life shared gratuitously by him, or they lessen it. That is, they either perfect him in much the same way (if I be permitted to use the analogy) as musical exercises bring a person to musical perfection, or else they corrupt him and diminish his human being and life and radically destroy the very germs of divine life communicated to us in grace and by the infused virtues.

Now, as a theologian using my reason and seeking the reasons of God's law, I reach this point of view. First of all, an action of its very nature is liable to corrupt my very being because of its very nature; by its very tendency, as act, it is disordered and corruptive, that is, by reason of its tendency towards such and such a moral object (for instance, *sumere aliena invito domino*), which is objectively already in disharmony with the rule of morality, with both the supreme rule or the eternal law known to me as a rule of human actions only supernaturally or by divine revelation [46] and with the proximate rule or right human reason, which is right only in so far as it is in conformity with the *regula suprema*.[47] This, as I see things, is nothing more than

[46] Cf. St Thomas, *S. theol.*, II, II, 8, 3 ad 3.

[47] Cf. St Thomas, *S. theol.*, I, II, 19, 4 ad 3; II, II, 154, 2 ad 2; *QDisp. de Malo*, q. 2, art. 4; *QDisp. de Veritate*, q. 17, art. 5 ad 4; *III Sent.* dist. 23, q. 1, art. 1, edit. Moos, n° 23-4.

the *conversio ad obiectum malum*; and in that consists most formally, for the theologian who scrutinizes the reality of sin scientifically, the very notion or *ratio* of sin.

However, since this action is of its very nature, that is, intrinsically and positively, already objectively constituted in evil and positively corruptive of human goodness, two things follow. Firstly, there is of necessity a turning away from the rule of reason (either alone or as illumined by faith)[48] and a consequent diminishing of the splendour of reason in human life.[49] This is the aversion directly and immediately consequent upon and caused by the original disordered conversion.[50] Secondly, there is of necessity a turning away from the *lex aeterna* and from the eternal Law-giver, who never forbids anything except that which does harm to us his creatures, made to his image and likeness.[51] This is a second aversion following upon and ultimately caused by the first. The intimate connection between the two, and implicitly the intimate connection between the sapiential and scientific functions of theology, between the judgment of reason and the convictions of faith, are succinctly put by St Thomas when he says that it is the same thing to despise the dictate of right reason and the law of God.[52]

[48] Cf. St Thomas, *QDisp. de Malo*, q. 8, art. 2; *S. theol.*, I, II, 59, 4; II, II, 136, 1, together with commentary of Cajetan; II, II, 124, 1 etc.

[49] Cf. above note 19.

[50] Cf. St Thomas, *Q.Disp. de Malo q.* 8, *art.* 2 *ad* 12: *Omne peccatum est aversio ab incommutabili bono et conversio ad commutabile bonum*; and IV Sent. dist. 16, q. 3, art. 2, qla 1 ad 2: *Ex inordinata conversione ad commutabile bonum redditur actus improportionatus ad conversionem ad finem. Et ideo fundamentum aversionis est conversio in peccato.* St Albert puts this more forcibly still when he writes: *Licet peccatum penes aversionem solam consideratum nihil sit, tamen non est omnino nihil secundum quod aversio substantificatur in conversione* (in *II Sent.* dist. 42, art. 2 ad 4, edit. Borgnet, t. 27, p. 656 b).

[51] See above note 29.

[52] St Thomas, *S. theol.*, I, II, 19, 5 ad 2. In this connection and as illustrative of all that has been said above, the following remarks of St Thomas, picked at random from different contexts, may be of interest: . . . *cum nihil aliud sit peccare quam transgredi divina mandata* (*S. theol.*, I, II, 109, 4); *peccare nihil aliud est quam recedere ab eo quod est secundum naturam* (*ibid.* I, II, 109, 8); *peccatum in humanis actibus est quod est contra ordinem rationis* (*ibid.*, II, II, 153, 2); III, CG, ch. 2, arg. 6: *peccatum non invenitur nisi in his quae sunt propter finem.*

THE NEED FOR REPENTANCE

From what has been said above about the true notion of sin in its theological context, we can without much difficulty deduce a correspondingly true notion of sorrow or repentance. First of all, it must be noted that without sorrow or repentance there can be no forgiveness of sin. That is the solemn teaching of the Council of Trent.[53] It is also the teaching of the Council of Trent that perfect sorrow or repentance can be present without and before the actual reception of the sacrament of penance and that this sorrow, in virtue of the love of God which informs it, can bring about full remission of sin.[54]

The distinction between perfect and imperfect repentance or sorrow is based on the double aspect of sin elaborated above. Should our attention be focused on the fact that, through our sin, we have gone against the will of God, who in his love and solicitude desires our good and perfection and through that his own glory, then our sorrow flows from a love of God as he is good in himself, infinitely deserving of our gratitude, obedience and love in return. And since we have failed in that wilfully, we are pained and turn away from sin and our evil ways and seek to make amends. That is perfect sorrow or repentance. Should our attention, however, be focused on the harm we have done ourselves and on the consequent danger we run of incurring the penalty of eternal damnation (brought on ourselves and inflicted by God in all justice, as we attempted to explain above),[55] then our sorrow flows from a certain love of self[56] and is rooted in a certain salutary fear of punishment. It is a true sorrow, a supernatural sorrow and is a real disposition to perfect sorrow.

[53] *Denz.* 1676.

[54] *Denz.* 1677.

[55] Cf. above note 21; also St Thomas, *Comp. theol.* I, ch. 172; St Augustine, *Conf.* I, ch. 12, PL 32/670: *Jussisti Domine et sic est ut omnis inordinatus animus sibi ipsi sit poena.*

[56] It should be noted here that divine charity has a double object: it is first of all our own completion in being, insofar as we are the image of God (that is the intrinsic objective final end of man); and then it is God himself as the object of our friendship (that is the extrinsic objective final end of man: cf. *S. theol.*, II, II, 23 1).

Together with the sacrament of penance it leads to full remission of sin and to perfect justification.[57]

If we attempt to analyse phenomenologically and theologically the notion of repentance we find first of all that it is something quite distinct from regret. Regret alone does not include the intention of making good the damage done either to ourselves or to God. It is a kind of fatalistic attitude of soul. Damage has been done; that we realize. But we decide that nothing can be done about it and leave it at that. On the other hand, we must carefully distinguish true repentance from remorse which leaves the sinner, while being fully conscious of his fault, overwhelmed, as it were, by it. It may even lead to despair which does not count on the possibility of forgiveness.

In between these two extremes there is to be found true sorrow or repentance. First of all, a sincere recognition of sin is required, without which the way to true and full repentance has not even begun. Then a certain turning away from sin (for one or other of the motives mentioned above) sets in, a change of heart, a detaching of oneself by mind and heart from one's fault. Upon this follows a sincere decision to have done with sin, a sincere intention, that is, of sinning no more.[58] This presupposes that one feels hurt or pained by the sin committed. Informing all and setting all this process in motion is hope or trust, the basis of our certainty that our sin can be forgiven and that God in his goodness is willing to forgive us and welcome us again into his friendship. We have only to recall and meditate on the parable of the prodigal son [59] to see how all these elements are contained there. At the end of the second century the Rabbi Simeon ben Halaftha described most beautifully the difference between the sinner coming to ask pardon of God and a defaulter seeking justice in a human court. Commenting on *Proverbs* 28: 13, 'He that covereth his transgressions shall not prosper,' he writes:

[57] Cf. *Denz.* 1678. Also St Thomas, *S. theol.*, III, 86, 3 ad 1.
[58] Cf. St Thomas, *III CG*, ch. 158 *per totum* together with corresponding places in the *Summa Theologiae* and his commentary on the fourth book of the Sentences.
[59] *Luke* 15.

'This is like the robber who is being tried before the questionarius; so long as he contradicts, he is beaten; but when he confesses, he receives his punishment. With God it is different. So long as the sinner does not confess, he is punished, but is discharged as soon as he has confessed, as it says, "But whoso confesseth and forsaketh them shall obtain mercy".'[60]

We do not have to go far to find our Lord's most explicit teaching on the structure and constitutive elements of repentance. He came on earth to save sinners, to save those who were lost;[61] and he spared no effort to bring home to his hearers what is required of them in order to obtain mercy and pardon of God the Father in heaven. Recognition of sin and open confession of fault is the first requisite; then a humble asking of pardon must follow in the assurance that God our Father is waiting to welcome us back to him. Then our Lord lays down two conditions for forgiveness which no theological analysis of repentance may omit or neglect. Firstly, in order to obtain pardon from God we must be ready to forgive our fellowmen, and be merciful to them. He put that condition of forgiveness into the prayer he taught us to say: 'Our Father, who art in heaven . . . forgive us our trespasses, as we forgive them that trespass against us.'[62] He expresses the same condition more forcibly still in the parable of the unmerciful servant: 'It is thus that my heavenly Father will deal with you, if brother does not forgive brother with all his heart.'[63] These are strong words and there is no mistaking their meaning. We are meant either to take them or to leave them. Secondly, we are taught by our Lord that God's forgiveness and welcome is not forthcoming unless we are ready to forgive those who have positively offended us and done us an injustice.[64] We cannot be at peace with God unless we sincerely strive to be at peace with our neighbour.

[60] Quoted in A. Büchler, *Studies in Sin and Atonement in the Rabbinic Literature of the First Century* (OUP, London, 1928), 345.
[61] Cf. *Luke* 5: 32; *Matt.* 9: 13; *Mark* 2: 17.
[62] *Matt.* 6: 12.
[63] *Matt.* 18: 35.
[64] Cf. *Matt.* 5: 23.

Repentance, then, has many faces and forms. It takes possession of the soul once we have realized that the love of God has been thwarted and that we have in some way pained him; once we realize that we have damaged his image in ourselves, in which likeness and similitude the perfection of our own being and life consists. Repentance engages or involves the whole man, and leads to a full turning of ourselves to God in service and in love.

I may be permitted to terminate these reflections on sin and repentance by quoting the warning of Rabbi Eliezer ben Hyrkanos writing towards the middle of the first century: ' Turn back a day before thy death.' When asked by his followers whether a man knew the day of his death to be able to act on that warning his reply was: ' All the more should he repent today, as he may die tomorrow; repent tomorrow, as he may die after tomorrow, and the result will be that he will have repented all his days.' [65]

[65] Quoted in A. Büchler, *op. cit.*, 348.

SELECT BIBLIOGRAPHY

Braun et al. — *Morale Chretienne et Requetes Contemporaines*, (Symposium) Tournai, 1954

W. D. Davies — *The Setting of the Sermon on the Mount*, Cambridge, 1964

Delhaye et al. — *Théologie du Péché* (Symposium) Tournai, 1960

C. H. Dodd — *Gospel and Law*, Cambridge, 1951

Josef Fuchs — *Theologia Moralis Generalis*, Rome, 1963

Id. — *Natural Law A Theological Investigation*, Dublin, 1965

Gerard Gillemann — *The Primacy of Charity in Moral Theology*, London, 1959

Edouard Hamel — *Loi Naturelle et Loi du Christ*, Bruges-Paris, 1964

Bernhard Häring — *The Law of Christ*, I, II, Cork, 1961, 1963

Id. — *Christian Renewal in a Changing World*, New York, 1965

Häring et al. — *Studia Moralia*, (Symposium) Rome, 1963

Rudolf Hofmann — *Moraltheologische Erkenntnis- und Methodenlehre*, Munich, 1963

Jacques Leclercq — *L'Enseignement de la Morale Chretienne*, Louvain, 1951

P. A. Liege — *What is Christian Life?* London, 1961

D. J. McCarthy — *Treaty and Covenant*, Rome, 1963

Engelbert Neuhäusler — *Anspruch und Antwort Gottes*, Düsseldorf, 1962

Marc Oraison — *Une Morale Pour Notre Temps*, Paris, 1964

S. Pinckaers — *Le Renouveau de la Morale*, Paris, 1964

Karl Rahner — *The Dynamic Element in the Church*, London, 1964

Id. — *Nature and Grace*, London, 1963

Virgil Redlich (Ed.) — *Moralprobleme im Umbruch der Zeit*, Munich, 1957

J. Regnier — *What is Sin?* Cork, 1961

Rudolf Schnackenburg — *The Moral Teaching of the New Testament*, London, 1965

Anselm Schulz — *Nachfolgen und Nachahmen*, Munich, 1962

Ceslaus Spicq — *St Paul and Christian Living*, Dublin, 1964

Id. — *Agape in the New Testament*, I, London, 1963

Fritz Tillmann — *The Master Calls*, London, 1962

Id. — *Handbuch der Katholischen Sittenlehre*, III, IV, Düsseldorf, 1963

V. Warnach — *Agape, Die Liebe als Grundmotiv der neutestamentlichen Theologie*, Düsseldorf, 1951

CAHILL AND CO. LTD., PARKGATE PRINTING WORKS, DUBLIN